You Can Retire
While You're Still Young Enough to Enjoy It

YOU CAN RETIRE

While You're Still Young Enough to Enjoy It

Les Abromovitz

DEARBORN™
A **Kaplan Professional** Company

Editorial Director: Cynthia Zigmund
Managing Editor: Jack Kiburz
Project Editor: Trey Thoelcke
Interior Design: the dotted i
Cover Design: Jody Billert

Published by Dearborn
a Kaplan Professional Company

Printed in the United States of America

99 00 01 10 9 8 7 6 5 4 3 2

Library of Congress Cataloging-in-Publication Data
Abromovitz, Les.
    You can retire while you're still young enough to enjoy it /
Les Abromovitz.
        p.   cm.
    Includes index.
    ISBN 0-7931-3017-4 (pbk.)
    1. Early retirement—United States. 2. Retirement—Planning. I. Title.
HD7110.5.U6A3 1999
332.024'01—dc21   98-53432
                                                                    CIP

DEDICATION

≈

Early retirement will be even sweeter, if you have a special person in your life with whom to share it. Hedy has been that person for me through 25 wonderful years of marriage. And to our favorite retirees, Belle and Jack Abromovitz, and Rae and Lou Gruenebaum, our parents.

CONTENTS

≈

PREFACE
≈

$\mathbf{A}$s you're waiting for your car pool, bus, or train to work on a subzero February morning, perhaps you dream about a time when your day isn't planned by your employer. Even when the weather isn't so frightful, there are a thousand other places you'd rather be than work. Or perhaps, you're in the middle seat in cattle class on a seemingly endless business flight. Whether you're in the air or on the ground, there's always too little time with the people you care about most and no time for yourself.

It doesn't have to be that way. You can retire early. You can choose how to spend each day. If that's your dream, you've picked up a book that can help make it a reality.

A wise person once said that a dream is a goal with a deadline. You can realize the dream of early retirement, long before the typical deadline of age 65. And you don't have to win the lottery or live like a miser to make it happen.

This book will show you how to reach the goal of early retirement, if that's what you really want. You'll learn to use the latest changes in the tax laws to your advantage, such as the $500,000 tax break on the sale of your home. You'll get the scoop on Roth IRAs and other retirement accounts. You'll find out how to tap your IRAs and 401(k) retirement savings plans without a penalty before age 59½.

Even if you've done a poor job of saving so far, you can still catch up and retire early. This book can help you identify ways to save money effortlessly and make shrewd investments for retirement. You'll read about potential sources of income you never knew existed. As you develop a strategy to make your dream a reality, you'll discover that early retirement may not be as far off as you think.

It's not enough to be financially ready for early retirement. You must also be ready for the psychological issues you'll face when you stop working. Many extremely difficult lifestyle choices affect whether you're able to retire early. As you read this book, you'll realize there are numerous retirement issues you've never even thought about but need to address before leaving the workforce.

If you want to work, work at a job you love, not one you'd love to leave. For many people, the decision to retire early doesn't mean they stop working. You can volunteer or find a job doing something meaningful, not just earning a paycheck. You'll be able to explore careers that are fun and creative, not boring and tedious. If you prefer, you can work a few hours each week in an exciting field or start a part-time business without the worry of making ends meet.

Even if you decide that early retirement isn't right for you, you'll put yourself on the right path to financial independence by reading this book. You'll be able to go to work, knowing you don't have to work. That knowledge makes most jobs a whole lot more enjoyable.

ACKNOWLEDGMENTS

≈

Many people have been extremely helpful in the preparation of this book. In particular, I would like to thank Cynthia Zigmund, Sandy Holzbach, and Trey Thoelcke of Dearborn, who've put up with my sense of humor, such as it is. I am also grateful to the folks in the art department at Dearborn, as well as everyone involved in the production of this manuscript.

≈ Whose Life Is It Anyway?

In the "Dilbert" comic strip, a woman complains about her job to Catbert, the evil human resources director. "I'm not enjoying my job," she says.

"Take this powerful antidepressant drug for the rest of your life," he advises.

"I didn't know H.R. could prescribe drugs," she replies.

"I'd hate to live in a world where that was illegal," Catbert says assuringly.

Perhaps, your own job makes you wish for antidepressant drugs. The thought of working at it for the next few decades is enough to put you under the sheets for a week. Your day-to-day work existence makes you question the meaning of life.

Worse yet, it's not just five days of work anymore. A *USA Today* story reports that employees are working more from home because of available technology, and they're also going into the office on weekends. A survey found that 73 percent of employees in offices of 100 workers or more do some weekend work. At some companies, it is not uncommon to find coworkers in the office on Sunday afternoon. After a week of meetings and phone calls, employees are using the weekends to catch up.

New technology has contributed to the number of extra hours that people are working. With access to e-mail and notebook computers, workers bring their jobs home with them. Their limited free time is cut into further by work at home or the necessary trip to the office to dig through piles of paperwork. Some can never catch up. There's always another deadline or new project that can't wait, or at least the boss thinks it can't wait.

Sometimes, the weekend is cut short by a business trip. Whether to save money or not waste a precious moment of the work week, your company may require you to leave on Sunday for business travel. Instead of spending Sunday evening at home with your family, you're off for another week of barely seeing them at all. Ironically, it's because of those family responsibilities that you lie awake wondering if you'll even keep your job.

Work might not be so bad if you can achieve some balance in your life. Whereas many companies talk a lot about wanting their employees to have a life, they take most of it. Another "Dilbert" cartoon shows Catbert talking to an employee. "Alice, the experts say you need to balance work and home life. You worked 80 hours last week. That's less than half of the hours in a week. Give us some balance, you selfish hag."

The stunned employee replies, "This conversation took a nasty turn."

Your employer's perception of balance, and your own, are often miles apart. Perhaps, your life would be a lot more enjoyable if you could limit your work week to 40 hours, not the number you're working now. Even if you put in a lot of hours, it would be nice to have peace of mind once you're home. Family members notice that distant look in your eyes as you remember some unpleasant experience that happened during the week or a distasteful task that awaits you on Monday. You'd give anything to not think of something you forgot to do or worry about a client who's never satisfied by the job you're doing.

A systems administrator complains that he didn't have such a great weekend. It was bad enough that he worked both days of the weekend. To make matters worse, the systems administrator woke up in the middle of night wondering if his equipment order was processed or lost.

As it stands your life is anything but perfect. How might you improve it? Start by asking yourself this question: What's my idea of a perfect day? Is it walking the beach at sunrise with a cup of coffee in your hand and the one you love by your side? Or is it waiting for the bus on a frigid winter morning, rushing so you won't be late for a job you've come to hate?

Obviously, that's a loaded question that begs for a particular answer. Maybe, your job isn't so bad and you don't mind the work or the commute. Nevertheless, it's not your idea of a perfect day. You'd like to get up in the morning and decide what to do without circumstances dictating your plans. Instead, the best you can hope for is a night swim or time to "veg out" in front of the television to help you unwind from a grueling day at work.

As you look up at the stars on a clear evening, you wonder how many days or years you have left on the planet and question whether it's worth settling for less than perfect days. You'd love to be in control of your universe, instead of depending on a paycheck that may end one day soon when your employer gets swallowed up by someone else's employer.

It's not the stars that determine your future. You can chart your own course to perfect days, or at least far fewer imperfect days than you have now. And you don't have to wait for the normal retirement age to have them. You can retire early and start seeing for yourself what constitutes a perfect day.

Some day there will come a time when your days are planned for you. There will be doctors appointments every other day or worse. Perhaps, you'll no longer feel comfortable behind the wheel and someone will need to drive you from place to place. Even if you can drive, it will become harder to get in and out of the car.

Before that time arrives, imagine what it would be like to choose how you'll spend each and every day. Maybe you'll take a day trip to an outlet mall, or just have a relaxing breakfast. Who knows? You might even get to read your morning paper in the morning instead of late at night. Some people just want to putter in the garden on a nice day or practice putting.

Many of us long for the freedom to just get in the car and go. There's a country song sung by Jo Dee Messina called "Heads Carolina, Tails California," that goes:

> Heads Carolina, tails California,
> Somewhere greener, somewhere warmer.
> Up in the mountains, down by the ocean,
> Long as I'm with you, it doesn't matter.

With the flip of a coin, you decide where you go that day with the special person in your life.

Though your odds are a lot worse when you play the lottery, the advertisements play to emotions that most of us feel. In one commercial for the Florida lottery, the winner spends his day fishing on a peaceful lake. In another, a couple talks about their life since winning the lottery. They describe the freedom and happiness they've gained. The wife observes that every day's a weekend.

When you're retired, it seems as if every day is a weekend. The only problem is that you've got to work for years to reach that point. For many people, retirement better not be like their weekends. If they're not working, many are running to the dry cleaner, chauffeuring the kids, or handling a thousand other errands they can't get to during the week.

Retirement at any age won't necessarily result in perfect days. Sometimes when you seize the day, as Robin Williams advised his students in *Dead Poet's Society*, you seize a rainy day. There will be days when it's going so badly, you'll look wistfully at the Prozac ad in a magazine. You won't be singing "Hakuna Matata," the song from *The Lion King* about having no worries.

Even in retirement, you'll never have a worry-free existence. Hopefully, however, you can reach a financial position where you won't worry about money. Though they may be financially ready to retire, as we discuss in Chapter 2, many people are never psychologically ready to retire. Some people will never enjoy life to its fullest, even if they're financially set and have all the time in the world.

Furthermore, retirement isn't the answer for many people. They enjoy their work and wouldn't know what to do with time on their hands. These people don't believe that the worst day at the beach is better than the best day at work.

LIFE BEYOND WORK

Most people have too many days ahead of them at work. And it's only going to get worse. In 1950, 87 percent of men age 55 to 64 were in the workforce. In 1997, it dropped to 68 percent. However, most analysts are predicting that there will be a reversal in the early retirement trend. A major reason is the decline in pensions that offer a defined monthly benefit and incentives to retire early. Another big reason will be the change in the official retirement age, which is defined as the time when full Social Security benefits are paid. Eventually, the official retirement age for younger baby boomers will be 67. Some experts say it will keep going higher.

Many analysts say that boomers will retire later because of financial circumstances. It doesn't have to be that way. You can retire early or find a lifestyle where work isn't an activity you dread. If you must work or want to work, it should be more than just the means to an end. And that end shouldn't require you to work until the traditional retirement age.

My wife and I love to drive the beach route from Fort Lauderdale to Boca Raton. We stop near Lighthouse Point at an inlet where boats go from the Intracoastal Waterway to the ocean. It's not unusual to find pelicans standing next to fishermen, waiting for their next handout. On one particular evening, a pelican was too tired to move from the entrance to the parking lot. A truck tried to get by him but the pelican wouldn't budge. The driver of the truck honked his horn but the pelican couldn't care less. The man got out of his truck and tried to shoo the pelican away. Finally, the pelican begrudgingly allowed the man to enter the lot. After doing so, the prehistoric-looking bird returned to his spot and put his head under his wing to get some shut-eye.

Not far from the inlet is a stretch of road called Hillsboro Mile. Some of the homes are priced in the neighborhood of $5 million. Nearby, however, you can get a condo for $50,000. And the residents of either get to come to the inlet for free.

Miles up the road on A1A is the town of Gulf Stream, which has been written up in *Worth* magazine as one of the most expensive places to live in the United States. Former president George Bush visits friends there from time to time. A short distance away is the Briny Breezes Trailer Park which abuts the ocean. Most residents believe they live in paradise.

Sure, it would be nice to be able to retire early and live in a mansion on Hillsboro Mile or in Gulf Stream. But life isn't so bad if you can retire early and live in a secure place where the ocean breezes come through your window every night and pelicans cause the traffic jams. Maybe, a condo in the mountains is your dream environment. If skiing from dawn to dusk is all you ask from life, an A-frame in the woods might be your paradise.

DREAMING ABOUT EARLY RETIREMENT

It's nice to dream about early retirement. Americans do it all the time. According to the seventh annual Retirement Confidence Survey conducted by the Employee Benefit Research Institute, two-thirds of workers would like to retire before age 65. One-third of that group would like to retire by age 55. But only 15 percent really expect to retire that early. That's not too surprising, considering that only 27 percent have any idea how much money they will need to retire.

Americans have a lot of excuses for not planning for retirement. The most common excuse is that workers cannot save more than they are currently saving. For many, retirement is too far off to plan for, so they don't bother. Some don't even have the time to calculate how much they'll need in retirement. A small percentage are afraid of the answer. A few believe the process is too complicated.

Well, you've picked up this book and that's a start. But it's just one baby step toward making your dreams a reality. A more significant step is to stop making excuses and move toward the goal of early retirement.

An editorial cartoon contains the caption, "Baby Boomers Finally Retire on Their Savings." In the cartoon, the husband declares, "This digital home theater with surround sound is the best investment we ever made, isn't it, Heather?" The wife in the cartoon asks if the husband wants more dog food to eat while they're watching the movie.

Economist Juliet Schor has written two books that address many of the issues you'll need to face as you plan for early retirement. *The Overworked American* deals with the long hours that many people put in at work. Schor followed that book with *The Overspent American,* which takes note of the work-and-spend lifestyle of many people. Schor discovered families earning more than $100,000 per year who feel they can't afford to buy everything they need. Schor observes that with many people who spend too much, wants quickly become necessities.

Overworked Americans are likely to stay overworked, if they continue to overspend. It's a lifestyle choice that can keep you in the workforce for years to come. The decisions you make today will either haunt you or thrill you decades from now. The choice is yours.

MAKING DREAMS A REALITY

In an episode of *The Wonder Years,* Kevin Arnold's father is having a bad time at work. After another terrible day, his wife asks him, "How was work?" He answers, "Work is work," which captures the way many people feel about the daily grind. Young Kevin wants to understand what his father does for a living and joins his dad at work. He watches his father deal with problem after problem and get screamed at by the boss.

That evening, Kevin asks his dad how he ended up being a manager at the company. With resignation, his father relates that he really wanted to be a sea captain but wound up in the job he has now. He tells his son, "You can't have every silly thing you want in life. You have to make choices."

Although you can't have every silly thing in life you want, some are yours for the taking. Early retirement involves many choices that are difficult to make. Your ability to retire early is dependent on the decisions you make about your lifestyle. Our first home cost less than $48,000. If we had never moved up, my wife and I probably could have retired at 35. The mortgage payment was $308 per month and the taxes were about $1,200 per year at the time.

Like most people, we wanted to improve our lifestyle. We dreamed of a bigger and better home. Then we wanted a second home in Florida. All the pieces were in place for us to retire at 40. We took time off from work for about 18 months. That's when we realized that we wanted to work but in a field that interested us. Our goal was to be challenged and like what we were doing each and every day. Financially, we would rather make $1,000 a month at something we enjoy doing than make $5,000 per month at a dull and boring job.

Once again, we both found positions that were new and different. The pay was better than we hoped and we had the opportunity to work in Florida near the beach. Because we were spending more time in Florida, our small vacation home no longer met our needs. We bought a single-family home, and began working out of financial necessity again.

Though work became a necessity, our parameters were the same. We would rather make less money at something rewarding than much more money in a position we hate. Although our new home was a step up, we were not overextended to a point where we had to take the higher-paying job. Our lifestyle has always been less than our income.

When you're ready to retire, permanently or temporarily, you face choices that can delay the event. Moving in and out of retirement isn't easy. It's harder to find a job each time, especially if you want a responsible position and your marketable skills aren't all that unique.

You also face choices that are difficult to make. We could have retired earlier by selling or renting our northern home, but we can't bear the thought. We don't want to rent the new Florida home either, which is why unconditional retirement won't be feasible for another few years. In our perfect retirement scenario, we're able to spend six months in Pittsburgh and six months in Florida. Take a wild guess which months we want to spend in the north and which we want to spend in the south.

Perhaps, you're more flexible than we are. Maybe you're willing to rent your dwelling while you visit exotic places in retirement or drive a Winnebago across the country. If your needs are simple, retirement can come much sooner than you hoped and before it's too late.

Choices about retirement are especially difficult because you learn more with each new experience. You may realize that the place you've chosen to retire in isn't all it's cracked up to be. It may have seemed ideal as a vacation retreat, but it just doesn't work as your full-time home. As we found, you may discover that vacation homes aren't necessarily adequate for full-time living, especially if you're used to more space.

Our coach home in Boca Raton, Florida, was ideal as a vacation home. For seven years we loved staying there instead of a hotel. We kept enough clothes and toiletries there to avoid having to pack for our trip. We were able to overlook the cramped quarters and the close proximity of the neighbors. As we spent more time there, however, it grew tougher to ignore the sound of a neighbor with prostate problems urinating in the middle of the night and people blocking our driveway with their cars.

Working instead of playing in that environment also exacerbated the space problems. With my wife working every day, she needed more clothes than the few we kept at the house. We quickly outgrew the small cupboards. In addition, there was no room for my files or reference books.

Even if you're comfortable with your living environment, your outlook on retirement may fluctuate from day to day.

Your spouse or loved one may not share your views. You might find that spending more time together doesn't help your relationship. In addition, the hobbies you enjoy may not hold the same appeal once you're involved in them more frequently.

For most people, attitudes toward work are sometimes in a state of flux. When you like your boss and enjoy your work, retirement isn't on your mind constantly. When work is driving you crazy, thoughts of retiring come frequently. The key is making certain you want to retire rather than just change jobs. Your dream of early retirement shouldn't be predicated on getting away from a nasty supervisor or a work situation that's unpalatable.

Even if you're absolutely certain it's retirement you're craving, there will be days when your choice seems wrong. Many new retirees have difficulty adjusting to their new lifestyles. You might even find that you miss your job or coworkers, even though that prospect seemed impossible.

Another consideration is your spouse or loved one's ability or desire to share in your retirement dream. If that special person stays in the workforce by choice or to reach an employment milestone, it's going to be extremely difficult for you. Walking the beach alone won't be the same. If your dream involves activities you engage in together, your plan has to include both of you retiring together. Just make sure you're both ready for retirement. If either of you feels you've made the wrong choice, the time spent together won't be as pleasant.

My wife and I have always been on the same page when it comes to decisions about retirement. We're very comfortable with our lifestyle, even though it's not right for everyone. Except for our houses, we don't live a very lavish lifestyle. Some of our friends laugh because we can almost always be found eating before six at one of the many restaurants with early bird specials in South Florida. They joke that we're the youngest people in the restaurant and the older folks call me "sonny." If these are the sacrifices we must make to be financially independent, it's fine with us.

We work, but the work has to meet certain parameters. We have to like the work and the people. It has to be creative and fun for us. If it isn't, we'll stop. Semiretirement is probably a better term for what we do now.

This book talks a great deal about retiring early, but not necessarily retiring from the workforce. Many people want to retire early, so they can pursue other careers, without money being a consideration. They can choose a livelihood without worrying how they'll live on what they're earning. While you may not want to be a sea captain like Kevin's dad, especially after seeing *Titanic*, there's still time left to pursue your dreams.

Working Woman magazine ran a piece called a "Guide to Early Retirement." The editor-in-chief of the magazine commented that the seemingly uncontroversial article generated some behind-the-scenes argument. Several editors lobbied against the article, arguing that the workaholic, free-spending boomers don't want to retire early. These fifty-something baby boomers, according to the editors opposed to the article, have another 30 to 40 years of high-octane fuel in reserve.

Maybe you don't have another 30 to 40 years of high-octane fuel in reserve. Perhaps, you don't have enough fuel to last the week, let alone several decades. The editor-in-chief of the magazine was only in her thirties, but she was already calculating and recalculating an early retirement. She was tired of being a slave to a paycheck and train schedules.

Smart Money magazine questioned if early retirement was an impossible dream. The magazine correctly pointed out that there are no easy answers, quick fixes, or magic formulas, and it is correct. There is no right answer or one strategy for every reader of this book. Instead, there are strategies and various routes that you can take to make that dream a reality.

Always remember that these are your dreams to either pursue or not pursue. The purpose of this book isn't to talk you into retiring early. It's to help you decide if early retirement is really what you're longing for, and how to make it possible if that's what you really want.

Dawn Steel, the first woman to run a major motion picture studio, subscribed to the philosophy, "Work to live, not live to work." Sadly, not long after writing those words in her autobiography, Steel died of a brain tumor.

Rules of the Road to Early Retirement

▶ The road to early retirement is going to involve many choices about lifestyle. Ask yourself whether you're content with your current standard of living or if you're still planning to move up. There are ways to move up and still move forward toward the goal of early retirement.

▶ Write down your dreams and see if early retirement is part of the scenario. If there's someone special in your life, make certain you're working toward the same goals.

2

≈ ## Are You Sure You Want to Retire Early?

You're sitting at a Jimmy Buffett concert, dreaming about living in Key West, not going to work tomorrow morning or ever again. The songs take you to places where aggravation seems a million miles away. He sings about margaritas, tropical breezes, and a cheeseburger in paradise. For you, paradise is anywhere but the job you're expected at tomorrow at 8:00 AM.

For most people, paradise is a place with no alarm clocks and no job that keeps you up nights. There are no deadlines, artificial or real. There are no bosses that make Dilbert's look like Mother Teresa. You don't need a Tylenol PM to get to sleep or Pepto Bismal to coat your stomach lining.

Unfortunately, even in paradise, there's aggravation. Two dozen houseboats moored in Key West found themselves being pushed out of Cow Key Channel. The owners of the houseboats claimed that developers were behind the movement to get rid of Houseboat Row. The residents, some of whom raise their children on these houseboats, argued that their laidback, bohemian lifestyle is being threatened by those who hope to build upscale hotels and condos.

At a condominium near Davie, Florida, the president of the condo is in a battle with a resident that makes the local newspaper. The resident, who has a back problem, wants to sit on an inner tube at the condo development's pool. He has a doctor's note and contends he keeps the inner tube in a corner of the pool. The condo president contends that the association's rules prohibit inner tubes in the pool, regardless of the reason. The large inner tube, the condo president argues, violates the rules.

No matter which side you agree with, the point is that even paradise can be aggravating. Although you may live in a dream environment, there are nightmares at times. Sometimes, the nightmares are people or situations that you can't avoid. Even if you aren't looking for a fight, a fight sometimes comes looking for you.

Some people thrive on controversy and a good fight. Others walk away from confrontation. One neighbor thinks about serving on the condo association board, but says he'll have another heart attack if he does. Another man in a different neighborhood enjoys serving on the homeowners association board. He spends part of the year in Boca Raton and the rest at his home in Vail, Colorado. Serving on the board adds meaning to his life, not aggravation.

No matter where you live, life outside work can be aggravating. It finally dawns on you, after three months, that AT&T has changed its rate structure for long-distance calls. For months, you've been waiting until after 5:00 to get the evening rate on toll calls. Unfortunately, unknown to you, AT&T has changed the rules and the daytime rate now extends from 7:00 AM until 7:00 PM.

After your discovery, you wait on hold for 30 minutes for AT&T's customer service. You're informed by a not-very-pleasant individual that you were notified at some point of the change in billing structure, but she's not sure how or when. Because a dozen other people you know are also unaware of the change, you surmise that the notification came on page 16 of your bill in the smallest of small print. One AT&T employee suggests that the notification was made in the newspapers, not in your phone bill. Glutton for punishment, you ask to speak to a supervisor who makes a guest appearance after another 15 minutes on hold. The supervisor, who is unaware of the change, puts you on hold until it's time to hang up and fight the good fight another day.

Even in retirement, there will always be AT&T and customer service people from hell. The only difference is that you won't be wasting your employer's time while calling and being frustrated. You'll be aggravated on your own time and it may be harder to take your mind off of the situation. And if you are the type who is easily agitated, retirement will not be free of aggravation or stress.

While Jimmy Buffett might recommend a margarita, a variation of a different song might work too: Don't worry. Be mellow. But that's easier said than done. You can never retire from life's aggravation.

RIGHT AND WRONG REASONS FOR RETIRING EARLY

A doctor writes to the newspaper to say he's retiring. Practicing medicine isn't what it used to be, he claims. According to the physician, managed care has ruined the practice of medicine. He's tired of fighting with insurance companies over every test he conducts and has grown weary of their meddling into his choice of treatment for his patients.

A dentist is experiencing the same burnout. After several decades of practicing dentistry, managed care has cut into his practice. He loses patient after patient to dentists who are on the list of preferred providers for the employers in his area. Although his overhead and expenses have risen, the fees he is paid for his services have been drastically reduced. He finds himself thinking more and more about retirement.

We don't know if either doctor followed through on his retirement. In either case, it's probably a bad idea. If the advent of managed care is the only reason either has for wanting to retire, there are probably other options. Let's face it. There are undoubtedly thousands of people in the managed care field who want to retire too.

Author Gail Sheehy has written about what she calls, "male manopause." Among other changes, work satisfaction decreases as men reach their fifties. They become increasingly intolerant of office politics. In their sixties, men have a desire to redirect experience and professional abilities, rather than retire.

Whether you're a man or a woman, don't forget that a lot goes on psychologically and physiologically as you age. Chucking it all is not a spur-of-the-moment decision. It's something to think about every day for years, not just after a bad day. The preparatory steps toward early retirement take years, so there will be plenty of opportunities to turn back or go off in a different direction.

To help decide if retirement is the right answer for you, look at what you'll miss and what you won't miss about your job. Make a list if it helps. Maybe you'll miss lunches on the expense account, but you won't miss working through lunch. Depending on your perspective, maybe you'll miss the business trips and the frequent flyer miles. Others won't miss being away from home, living out of a suitcase, rushing to the airport, overbooked flights, and eating dinner alone.

There are pros and cons that must be considered. You won't be stuck in the middle seat on last-minute business flights, but you'll also lose your airline club membership. You'll be free to hit the open road at any time, but you lose the company car. There will be more time to golf, but no golf outings that you can put on the expense account.

Perhaps, you'll miss the comaraderie of the people in your office. Or maybe there are just too many bosses who don't seem to know what they're doing. The 401(k) retirement savings plan is great, but there are 401 assignments due at once.

Maybe, you're feeling too old for the commute, the weather, the pressure, the deadlines, the aggravation, the games, and the politics. Sure, you can stick it out, but why? You're starting to feel like one of those dinosaurs you joked about at an earlier stage of your career.

There are pros and cons to everyone's career, even the people at the top. The U.S. Trust Company polled corporate executives regarding the advantages and disadvantages of corporate life. They loved the fringe benefits and financial rewards. They didn't like not having time to relax or take vacations. These corporate executives felt they lacked the time to participate in sports or their hobbies. They were, however, pleased with the retirement benefits.

Retirement may be their first opportunity to take a care-free vacation. In a different survey conducted by an executive search firm in Cleveland, Ohio, 38 of 100 chief executives reported that they either canceled or shortened a family vacation within the past 12 months. A good guess is that an even larger percentage took work with them and called the office frequently.

BITTER PILLS TO SWALLOW

Early retirement involves a great many financial and emotional issues. If retirement isn't everything you want it to be, there is a chance you'll harbor bitterness toward your former employer. You shouldn't be retiring because of your hatred for that employer or disenchantment with your current career. If that's the case, you're approaching early retirement with the wrong attitude.

There's nothing wrong with wanting to retire early because there's no job out there that meets your needs. Early retirement allows you to explore other careers where you don't have to worry about how much you're being paid or whether you'll advance to the next step on the ladder. You'll look for jobs based on whether you like the people, the challenge, or the work itself. And when that particular endeavor no longer meets your needs, you'll move on.

Rather than seeking early retirement out of anger, it's better to be motivated by more positive emotions. Perhaps you want to volunteer for a position that pays nothing at all. Or maybe, you want to work at a hobby that may not produce financial rewards. Peace of mind comes from knowing you don't have to earn a buck from your activities.

My wife and I took a sabbatical from our careers in late 1992. Because both of our employers were downsizing, we were able to negotiate voluntary separation packages. We both left with a nice separation check. We left behind great friends who we still see from time to time. We left with pensions that we can draw on someday, as well as a lot of money in our 401(k) retirement savings plans.

We still have to work, unless we're willing to liquidate some of our assets, but we've gotten to pursue dreams like writing books for a living and working in television. Because we left on solid financial footing and things have worked out well, there's no bitterness toward our former employers. We felt we were treated fairly by our employers.

My 401(k) retirement savings plan was invested primarily in company stock, which has soared since I left. Who knows? Maybe there's a correlation between my leaving and the stock going up. I find that as the price of the stock goes higher, the fonder I am of my former employer.

If your anger at your employer is the reason you want to retire, you're in for trouble. You're likely to become more angry and bitter in retirement, especially if you feel short-changed by the quid pro quo for your years of service to the company. A few years after my wife left her employer of 19 years with the voluntary separation package, the company continued its downward spiral. Dozens of her friends left the company through no choice of their own. Thousands of employees lost their jobs and are extremely bitter about the way their careers ended. That's not the best start to early retirement.

RETIRING FROM STRESS

The long-term research seems to clearly indicate a relationship between occupational stress and heart disease. According to experts, those with the highest blood pressure and the highest risk of heart disease are those with the greatest responsibilities and the least control over their work.

USA Today followed six workers over the course of their day and monitored their blood pressure. One of the six workers commented that his regular job wasn't stressful. He found his part-time weekend job as a short-order cook caused more stress. Furthermore, he felt that his blood pressure went up after getting home to his wife and two young children.

A 59-year-old participant in the study gets up at 5:20 in the morning, drives to the train station, and is at his desk by 7:00. He handles very stressful duties for his brokerage house, skips lunch, and has 100 phone conversations each day. To top it off, his oldest son and daughter-in-law moved back in with him, along with their two babies, a dog, and a cat.

All of the persons observed had ways to cope with stress. Perhaps, there's another way. Leave that job behind, along with the stress that goes with it. As long as that's not going to produce financial worries and stress, it's an option to consider.

Retirement does not signal the end of stress and aggravation for everyone. Professor Virginia Richardson of Ohio State University conducted a study of 222 new retirees in Central Ohio. Her study found that retirement can increase stress instead of lowering it.

From Dr. Richardson's study, we learn that drinking can become a problem in retirement. Retirement gives people more opportunity to drink. The study also indicates that retirees shouldn't expect to travel constantly. The appeal of travel wears off. The expense of traveling is also a problem.

Hopefully, this book won't lead anyone to drink, including the author. Before we deal with the financial aspects of early retirement, it's important to consider the psychological problems you may encounter. In many instances, retirement living is more stressful for people, not less. Having more time on your hands frequently means you have more time to stew over the little aggravations that creep into your life. And if you're retired without a paycheck coming every few weeks, you may find yourself more aggravated by these situations. For many people, work takes their mind off annoying little problems. Of course, annoying little problems are often replaced by annoying big problems at work.

FINANCIAL INDEPENDENCE DAY

The people who make commercials seem to think a lot of us want the freedom to chuck it all. A Toyota commercial shows a car riding through city traffic with a surfboard on the roof. Even though it's Tuesday, the driver is headed for the water. The message from Toyota is that in their car, you can break the rules.

But most working people aren't breaking the rules. Instead, they're breaking their necks trying to get to work on time. They're driving through snowstorms or torrential rains, risking life and limb, to get to work. They race from the parking lot to the office building, huffing and puffing all the way. As they try to catch their breath, these aging baby boomers wonder if they'll make it anywhere but the emergency room.

In a radio commercial, a man with a gravely voice talks about getting too old to wake up at dawn and work out in the cold. He's worked hard all his life, earning a living with his hands, and he's getting too old for that. But as the commercial comes to an end, he talks about the satisfaction of using a great power tool to do his job well and he realizes he isn't too old. Not everyone gets that same sense of satisfaction from work. Many realize they're working exclusively for the money and don't get anything else from their job. Yet they're not sure if there's anything else they want to do.

Retirement may not be the answer for these people. They might only need a break from the workforce to recharge their batteries. George Costanza on *Seinfeld* only wanted a summer off, financed by his separation package from the Yankees. During the "summer of George," he planned to bite the fruit of life and let it drip down his chin.

A group of women in their thirties and forties were having lunch one day. Each was approaching a job change of some sort. Each was dreading it in some way. At first, the discussion led one to believe that none of them wanted to work. Upon closer analysis, however, the women seemed to be yearning for jobs with more flexibility and the ability to work at home from time to time.

Most men and women want that flexibility. Few people want to be shackled by a nine-to-five job that affords no time for anything but work. Along with flexibility, they want control over their work and how to structure it. If they can't have that, then many people want to retire.

Before we discuss the financial aspects of early retirement, it's imperative that you examine your motives and make certain what you want. There are other options available besides leaving the workforce cold turkey. Ultimately, if you're financially independent, you can choose the work situation that meets your needs.

WORKING BECAUSE YOU WANT TO, NOT HAVE TO

A woman writes to the advice column of a local newspaper. She's worried about her husband who's about to retire. The woman notes that he never developed any hobbies because he always worked so hard. She complains that he isn't interested in anything except sports and the stock market. Although they are financially comfortable, her husband doesn't want to travel or do much of anything. She fears he'll become like the husbands of her friends. They act like lost little boys, following their wives around and driving them crazy.

Unfortunately, neither Dr. Crane nor Dr. Hartley could solve this couple's problems. The advice from the columnist was that they should communicate more and he should consult in his former profession to remain active. If you're being dragged kicking and screaming into retirement, put this book back on the shelf. Readers who hope to retire early should be chomping at the bit for the day when they'll be able to work or play at any activity they choose.

Another couple squabbles about when and where they'll retire. She'd like to retire in her mid-fifties. The woman's husband doesn't appear to ever want to retire. She half-jokingly notes that his hero is a friend's father, who worked until well into his eighties.

From afar, you have to wonder if some people will ever be able to retire. The *ABA Journal* noted that U.S. Supreme Court Justice Ruth Bader Ginsburg takes a grocery sack full of mail and a small flashlight to the movies. It wasn't quite clear if she read her mail during the film or during the previews. With that type of work ethic, it may be extremely hard to retire at any age.

Wanting to retire early shouldn't make you question your work ethic. Most people don't know what it's like not to work. They've been working since their mid-teens, whether after school or from the moment they graduated. Although they're hard workers, the thought enters their minds that there has to be more to life than work. More than a few are workaholics, who spend 70 to 80 hours a week at their jobs.

Retirement isn't likely to change your work ethic. Initially, you'll feel guilty that you're not working every minute of every day. But as long as you're active, learning, and experiencing new things, you have nothing to feel guilty about. As we'll discuss later, many early retirees work part time. While it's doubtful they'll earn what they once did, that's only an issue if money is your sole criteria for valuing what you do. Unfortunately, many people only feel they're doing something useful when they get paid for it.

There will be bouts of depression. You may question the meaning of your life, now that work is over. Perhaps, you'll be disappointed that your career wasn't as successful as you imagined. Maybe, your career expectations were never fulfilled. A retired CEO of Westinghouse, which became CBS, expressed regrets about his career. Due to the problems that Westinghouse experienced, he felt his career was a waste.

Early retirement isn't about shattered dreams or unfulfilled expectations. It's about new dreams and new challenges. Sure, you'll be depressed from time to time, but a different kind of future awaits you. You're at a crossroads again and maybe the road you choose will lead somewhere new and exciting.

PSYCHOLOGICAL PROBLEMS OF EARLY RETIREMENT

As we move into the financial issues associated with early retirement, we'll end this chapter with a discussion of the psychological problems of early retirement. The biggest problem for many people is money. We all have our peculiarities when it comes to money. Some people are compulsive spenders and get an ego boost from buying things. Others enjoy the security of saving money and watching it grow. Some see an item they want and can't delay gratification for a moment. Others over-analyze purchases, wondering if it's a wise decision or if they can get a better price elsewhere.

Although few of us would object to being rich, most of us will be content with enough. Our needs are relatively simple. Few of us want to worry about money. We'd rather work at a job we don't particularly like than worry about money. Nevertheless, those who are willing to strive toward the goal of early retirement would rather have a lesser lifestyle than work or worry about money.

Shifting from a saving to spending mode may prove to be a difficult adjustment. You've probably spent a number of years in the workforce, building assets. Unless you're able to live without tapping the principal, you'll be depleting your assets rather than watching them grow. Even if you don't view yourself as materialistic, it's tough to change your perspective. Fortunately, it's not a change that has to happen overnight.

Sometimes, you become psychologically anchored to having X number of dollars in your checking account or a net worth of a particular amount. Even if you're absolutely certain you won't outlive your money, you don't like watching it go down. Until you're collecting a pension or Social Security benefits, you really won't be collecting the equivalent of the paycheck you're receiving now. You'll be drawing from your savings, rather than income, which is hard for some people to do.

Even if you have a strong self-image, don't minimize how much of your ego is dependent on work. If you worked hard to become a professional, it might be difficult to say you're retired. You might find yourself saying that you're a retired engineer or a retired architect. Or if you're like George Constanza, you can just lie and say you're an architect.

In addition, don't underestimate how much of your ego is tied to salary. As we'll discuss later, part-time work may be part of your strategy to retire early. And if you can't scrape by without working, a number of psychological issues may arise. Good part-time jobs are often harder to find than full-time jobs. Despite everything you've read, employers aren't waiting in line to hire seasoned people who were once executives or managers, unless their particular skills are in demand. And as those of us who read "Dilbert" know, executives and managers have no particular skills.

After you've been a rung or two up the corporate ladder, it's hard to go backwards, even if it's part time. At an upscale bookstore, a cashier addresses a couple who just walked in the store with their pet in hand. "I'm sorry, but dogs aren't allowed," he says to the customers in a very nice way. The couple becomes irate and badgers the poor sales clerk. They walk out in a huff and return a minute later. "We were going to buy $400 in Beanie Babies and you've lost that sale," they say loudly. Unconvinced, the clerk waves good-bye to them, then says to a fellow worker, "I don't have to take this crap for $6 an hour."

Unfortunately, with many part-time jobs, you take a lot of abuse for $6 an hour. The public often blames a cashier for long lines or the store's mismanagement. Even though that $6-an-hour employee is not part of management, he is the focal point of the public's anger.

The point is that you need to be psychologically prepared for the down side of any job, even a part-time one. Often, those jobs are harder and more frustrating than the one you have now. And you're getting paid a whole lot less to take the grief. Unless you're someone with a very thick skin, you won't be too keen on finding yourself in that situation.

Though retirement is the perfect time to find yourself and take stock of your life, you have to know yourself before you retire. You may be a negative person who frequently makes the worst of a situation. Or you may be the type who has dreams but always has an excuse for not attempting to realize them. Having too much time on your hands can become a procrastinator's dream.

As you plan for early retirement, you'll feel fear. Maybe you feel it now as you wonder if your job is secure. Retirement is an unknown and no matter how much you plan, you'll never really know how well it will work out.

Finally, it's important to consider the psychological value of work. Some people need the structure of going into the same place every day with the same people. Though they complain about the job and the people, not having that routine can damage them psychologically. For some reason, an active retirement lifestyle doesn't compare to climbing the corporate ladder or working. These people need a job far more than early retirement.

With the right psychological state of mind, everyone should be able to enjoy retirement. Whether you make it or not, you should be in better shape financially and psychologically for having tried to reach that goal. Knowing you're able to retire soon is as close as you can get to financial independence. Whether you retire early or not, you'll achieve peace of mind, knowing you control your destiny.

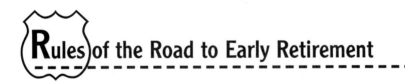

Rules of the Road to Early Retirement

▶ The desire to retire early is something you should feel, even when your career is going well. If it's not something that's always in the back of your mind, chances are you don't really want to retire.

▶ Life isn't without angst, even if you're retired and financially comfortable. For some people, having too much time on their hands isn't good for them.

▶ You are the one who can best judge how you'll react to the challenges that go hand-in-hand with early retirement. As you approach these issues, you must be totally rational and objective.

▶ Implementing an early retirement strategy can help you achieve financial independence, even if you never retire early. You'll have the freedom to work because you want to, not because you can't quit.

CHAPTER 3

≈ Working Out of Greed, Not Need

Maybe you can hang onto your job until the traditional age of retirement. You can go into the same place every day, see the same people, and do the same job. A coworker writes to a former coworker and tells her what she's missing. Everything's the same, he writes. George is George and Bob is Bob.

Many people like doing the same thing day after day. They hate and resist change. At a company that's been having financial problems for years, many employees live in fear of the day when the company will let them go. They've lived under the shadow of layoffs, yet they don't look elsewhere for a job.

The dream of early retirement isn't for anyone with an aversion to risk and change. Individuals like that usually want security at any price. For them, work is their lifeline. They wouldn't do well without a place to go to each morning.

If you enjoy your work and like being there every day, you're fortunate. Not everyone feels that way. For some the idea of a perfect day doesn't include a job they don't enjoy. Life for them is more than just a paycheck. It should be an adventure, not the same dull workday.

Previously, we discussed how retirement decisions are dependent on lifestyle choices. Most of us are accustomed to certain creature comforts. We like living in a certain neighborhood or a particular house. Many people feel strongly about driving a luxury car, rather than an inexpensive but reliable one. The following quiz is anything but scientific, but can help you determine if you're working out of greed or need:

Would you retire tomorrow if you

- had to give up the car you're driving now?
- needed to trade down to a less expensive home?
- won't be able to go out to dinner as much?

As much as people say they want to retire, many feel it isn't worth losing the luxuries they've come to enjoy.

Suppose you were forced to make the following decision: You can receive $30,000 per year and never work again or go to work every day and earn $60,000 per year. Obviously, a lot depends on how much you make now and what you need to sustain your lifestyle. For some, $60,000 wouldn't begin to meet their expenses and they have no desire to lower their lifestyle accordingly. On the other hand, others would find a way to get by on $30,000, if it meant being free from the pressures and constraints of their full-time job.

Even if you can survive on a small amount of money, no one's going to hand it to you. A commercial for SunAmerica, a financial services organization, shows a man going to a garage sale and buying a painting. Behind the painting is an original copy of the Declaration of Independence, valued at $2 million. In the commercial, dozens of other people are buying paintings, hoping they'll make a similar discovery. The voice-over cautions viewers that they can hope to get lucky or they can achieve financial security with the help of SunAmerica.

It is extremely sad to watch people who feel the lottery is their only hope for financial security. Even those of us who waste a dollar or two per month have a peculiar mind-set. We don't play the lottery when it's only $6 million. But when the jackpot reaches an extraordinary amount like $20 million, we stand in line to buy our ticket. It's almost as if $6 million is no big deal.

Most of us succumb to greed at times. I worked for a large financial services company for many years. My 401(k) retirement savings plan was primarily invested in stock, which has done quite nicely. Thanks to the skyrocketing price per share, there's more in the account than I ever expected. It's well above the price per share that I once said I would sell at if it came to pass. Yet, I can't bring myself to convert the shares to a fixed-income investment that is much less risky.

Perhaps, it's less greed than wanting to do the most with our money. We all think that we could retire comfortably on X number of dollars, but wouldn't it be great if we had a little more. We could live a little better in retirement.

The problem, however, is that decisions made out of greed can delay retirement until it's too late. A Merrill Lynch employee told me about having to work 20 more years to get the full value of the company's deferred incentive plan. Other people have confided that they're staying with an employer because it will mean a few dollars more in their monthly pension. However, these same people can get by nicely without those few extra dollars in their monthly pension—and retire earlier.

As I discussed in Chapter 2, attitudes toward money are very different. Two people can grow up in the same household but develop very different ideas about money. In one family, the older sister spends every penny she makes and isn't concerned about saving for the future. Meanwhile, her younger brother enjoys squirreling money away and hates tapping his nest egg for any reason.

Whether you want to retire early or not, this book can help you determine your attitudes toward money. Hopefully, it will at least get you thinking about how you'd like to spend the rest of your life.

PULLING THE PIN ON EARLY RETIREMENT

A recent best-seller, called *The Millionaire Next Door,* describes some of the traits millionaires have in common. Unlike the stereotype, millionaires don't always live lavish lifestyles and spend money without thinking.

Financial planner Alexandra Armstrong notes that although one-third of her clients are millionaires, they still have a cautious attitude about money. They ask critical questions before major purchases, which helps them realize that certain purchases aren't really necessary.

If you become overly cautious about money, you'll probably never buy anything. Similarly, you might never think you have enough. You'll look at your pension statement and say, "If I hang on three years longer, I'll get $200 more each month." And after those three years, you realize that you'll get a few dollars more each month you stay. With a little luck, you'll die at your desk and won't waste any money on retirement.

Obviously, I'm being facetious. The point is that most people eventually want to stop working and enjoy the fruits of their labor. But some people can't abandon those incredible saving habits they've cultivated over the years. Unless you want to die at your desk, you'll eventually need to pull the pin and retire. However, if you pull the pin at the wrong time the ramifications are quite serious.

In Chapter 7 we look at the new Roth Individual Retirement Accounts (IRAs). Unlike traditional IRAs, there are no forced distributions at age 70½. With a traditional IRA, the government forces you to begin withdrawing a percentage of your account at that age. In extolling the benefits of the Roth IRA, one financial writer was thrilled that you never have to withdraw from it until death.

Wow, there's a selling point. You can accumulate money for a lifetime and never spend it. If that thought is appealing, the dream of early retirement isn't for you. I hope readers of this book have more in mind than counting their money for the rest of their lives. If you retire early, the odds are good you'll need to spend part of that nest egg each year, rather than watching it grow for your heirs to enjoy.

EXIT, STAGE LEFT

The cartoon character Snagglepuss used to be fond of saying, "Exit, stage left." The purpose of this book is to help you exit the workforce while you're young enough to enjoy the years you have left.

By offering a strategy for exiting the workforce at an earlier stage in life, no inference should be made that the traditional retirement age is old. There are many people in that age group and older who are far more active and physically fit than most 40 year olds. The only point is that some people don't want to wait that long.

While there are many different stages of life, this book will only worry about two of them. For our purposes, there is the stage of life before age 59½ and the stage of life after age 59½. Before age 59½ is stage left. After age 59½ is stage right.

The post–59½ stage is closer to the traditional time of retirement. The Social Security Administration views 65 as the traditional age for retirement, but this will eventually move up to age 67. At that age, you'll be able to draw your full Social Security benefit. Perhaps, you'll have a pension that will kick in to supplement Social Security. You'll probably also need other sources of income to supplement your pension and Social Security check.

Age 62 is the magic number for some people. At that point, you might qualify for a smaller pension, along with a reduced Social Security check. Maybe, you can push up the retirement date even further. By investing heavily in IRAs and 401(k) retirement savings plans, you can prepare for the post–59½ stage of your life. At age 59½, you're free to withdraw from those retirement accounts without paying the 10 percent penalty that's usually applied. The same age requirement applies to annuities, which have long been viewed as a traditional investment for retirement.

Let's say you want to secure your post–59½ stage of retirement. You calculate that $600,000 in IRAs and 401(k) retirement accounts will do the trick. Suppose you can achieve an 8 percent rate of return with a modest amount of risk. If you have $300,000 at age 50½, your money will double and produce the necessary $600,000 by age 59½, even if you don't contribute another dime.

But suppose you can't wait to exit, stage right. You want to exit, stage left, before age 59½. If you've really built up enough money in your retirement accounts, you might consider accessing them before age 59½. Obviously, you don't want to get hit with a 10 percent penalty. You've worked too hard for that money to give it away. In Chapters 6 and 7, I'll be looking at ways to draw from your retirement accounts without getting nailed with penalties. There are ways to do it.

Despite the loopholes in the tax law, as a general rule, the funds you've put away for the second stage of retirement should not be used to make an earlier exit. You shouldn't be tapping your 401(k) retirement accounts before age 59½, unless you have far more than you'll need for later in life. IRAs are also intended to meet your retirement needs beyond age 59½.

If your post–59½ needs are met, you need cash during the transition period from your early retirement date until age 59½. Work backwards from age 59½ to determine the amount of cash you will need. With each year's worth of savings, you can move up your early retirement date.

Let's keep it simple. Suppose you have all the money you need for age 59½ and beyond in retirement accounts, along with your pension and Social Security. You have $40,000 in a money market account and with some belt-tightening, your family can live on $40,000 per year. Theoretically, you can now exit, stage left, one year before age 59½.

Still too long to wait? If it is, you'll need more funds set aside so you can move that date up. Carrying the calculations further, if you want to retire at 50, you'll need an available source of funds to take you from that age until 59½. Once again, if your family lives on $40,000 a year, you'll need roughly $360,000 after taxes to live on during the nine years until age 59½. Assuming your $360,000 is invested, the earnings will help you keep pace with inflation and will allow for some breathing room in your budget.

Obviously, there are many other tax, investment, and financial issues to consider and they will be addressed in later chapters. Furthermore, there are many other options aside from squirreling away thousands of dollars. In subsequent chapters, advice will be offered so you can exit, stage right or stage left.

Hopefully, you can take advantage of the Taxpayer Relief Act of 1997, which opens many roads to early retirement. In addition to the new Roth IRA, which will help solidify the post–59½ stage of retirement, there are exciting opportunities to help fund the pre–59½ stage of retirement. These tax breaks will help you build the cash needed to make the transition to the post–59½ stage of retirement.

Some of the possibilities include the new tax break on capital gains. Under the Taxpayer Relief Act of 1997, the top tax rate on long-term capital gains was reduced from 28 percent to 20 percent. For taxpayers in the 15 percent bracket, the top tax rate on long-term capital gains is now 10 percent. With the right investments and the favorable tax treatment under the new law, you might be able to build a nest egg for making that exit, stage left, before age 59½.

The new tax law also provides for an enormous tax break on the sale of your primary dwelling. You can make up to $500,000 profit, if you're married, and not pay federal income taxes. You no longer have to be 55 or older to qualify for a tax break. The profit on your home might supply the capital you need to leave the workforce early. But if you want to keep your home, don't despair. There are other ways to retire early without ever going through a stage in life when you're broke.

Outlined below are some of the possibilities for exiting the workforce, stage right or stage left.

Early Retirement Strategy

Exit, Stage Left *Financing Pre–59½* *Time Frame*	*Exit, Stage Right* *Financing Post–59½* *Time Frame*
Possibilities	Possibilities

- Retirement savings plans such as 401(k)s
- Tapping IRAs early
- Taking pensions early
- Savings
- Investments
- Tax-free proceeds from sale of primary dwelling
- Rental of primary dwelling or vacation home
- Part-time work

- Retirement savings plans such as 401(k)s
- IRAs
- Pensions
- Social Security
- Savings
- Investments
- Annuities
- Part-time work

ENOUGH IS ENOUGH

For some people, the answer is simple. They want to have enough. So when is enough, enough?

Financial expert Jonathan Pond advises that one of the most important determinations is how much of your nest egg you can safely withdraw. You risk running out of money if you take out too much. Pond advises that you shouldn't withdraw more than 7 percent of your investments during the first year of retirement, assuming you're retiring at 65. People who are retiring early shouldn't withdraw more than 6 percent the first year.

Once you have your bare bones budget established, you need to look at what figure permits you to withdraw 6 percent and still break even. You can increase your withdrawal rate if your investments are doing well.

Suppose it's not important to you to preserve your nest egg for your heirs. Your goal is to die broke, as the title of one financial book suggests. If you want to spend every penny, someone retiring today with $50,000 can withdraw $400 a month, every month, for 30 years. The figure presumes a 10 percent rate of return, which is doable if you stick with equity investments. If you don't achieve that rate of return and maintain the same level of withdrawal, you'll be broke even sooner.

Let's suppose you have $500,000, not $50,000. You can withdraw ten times that amount, or $4,000 per month for 30 years. And if you have $1,000,000, you can withdraw 20 times the $400, or $8,000 per month.

As you'll see in upcoming chapters, being rich on paper isn't necessarily the answer to early retirement. You can be a millionaire on paper and still not be able to retire. One problem is that you need liquid assets, not a home worth half a million dollars, even if you've paid off the mortgage. Or maybe you have $600,000 in retirement accounts that you can't touch until you're 59½, unless you're willing to pay a penalty. Being a millionaire on paper isn't the answer, unless a lot of your money is in cash, bonds, stocks, mutual funds, and readily accessible if you need it.

A financial planner in *The Wall Street Journal* compared two investors, each with $500,000. One has $500,000 in a taxable account and the other has $500,000 in a 401(k). The financial planner pointed out that the investors really don't have the same amount of money. The investor whose $500,000 is in a 401(k) still must pay taxes when the money is withdrawn. Similarly, if you own stock worth $500,000 but still must pay tax on the gain, you don't have as much as the person with $500,000 in an account on which the taxes have already been paid.

As you plan for early retirement, you'll need to finance both the pre–59½ stage of your life and the post–59½ stage. In each case, you need enough money after taxes to live on. The road won't be smooth or without risk. The good news is that there's more than one route to reach the goal of early retirement, if you don't like how long any one is going to take or the sacrifices that must be made. Hopefully, the directions will be clear, but only you can decide if the path is worth taking. At a minimum, the steps that follow can bring you closer to financial independence, even if independence from work isn't in the cards.

ROADMAP TO EARLY RETIREMENT

1. Determine your present financial situation.
2. Find out how much your present lifestyle is costing you.
3. Estimate how much your retirement lifestyle will cost.
4. Secure the pre–59½ and post–59½ stages of retirement. Identify ways to cut expenses from your present budget and save more. Along with putting away money in traditional retirement vehicles, start a fund that you can tap before age 59½.
5. Identify investments that will produce a greater rate of return.
6. Contribute as much as you can to 401(k) and similar retirement savings plans. Remember that equity investments will usually be best over the long haul.
7. Explore your IRA options and take advantage of the new Roth IRA or a traditional IRA.
8. Learn as much as you can about your company's pension plan, including when you're vested and how much you'll lose by taking it at a younger age.
9. Obtain an estimate of how much you'll receive from Social Security at age 62 and age 65.
10. Look into part-time work opportunities in a field you enjoy as a source of income until you're able to tap retirement accounts without penalty.
11. Evaluate your current housing situation and whether it's right for retirement. Consider whether you're willing to sell your house or rent it to finance an earlier retirement date.
12. Make absolutely certain you have guaranteed-renewable health insurance until you're covered by Medicare.

Most of us want financial independence for a reason. Maybe, we want to use our money to help others or just to help ourselves. We equate money with freedom. It gives us the ability to choose how we spend our time. Perhaps, you're like many people who have plenty of money to spend but little time to spend with their family or to enjoy life.

If you watch television in the middle of the night, the answers are all there. The infomercials can show you how to achieve financial independence and washboard abs. Personally, I'd trade financial independence for washboard abs, but that's just me. Maybe, the person on the psychic hotline will tell me when this is all going to happen. Hopefully, it will be before I've wasted hundreds or thousands of dollars.

In all seriousness, there are few shortcuts to financial security. In March of 1998, a promoter of get-rich videotapes was charged in a 90-count federal indictment. He is accused of defrauding the public and laundering $7 million. In his late night infomercials, he offered videotapes and books on how to make money by buying foreclosed properties. The infomercial guru also marketed the materials in seminars across the country.

There are few legal ways to make thousands in one day. The road to financial independence isn't an easy one. You have to work toward that goal every day. And if you don't, you won't be a step closer to early retirement.

There's a piece of exercise equipment sitting in our garage that I never use. It may work; it may not work. I'll never know because I never use it. We hang the laundry on it. Maybe I could have had washboard abs. I'll never know. Similarly, if you want to retire early you'll have to take those initial steps toward achieving the goal of early retirement.

Rules of the Road to Early Retirement

▶ Take advantage of the tax breaks offered by the Taxpayer Relief Act of 1997. The tax rate on capital gains has been lowered. The new Roth IRAs let you accumulate tax-free money for retirement.

▶ Look at retirement in two stages. The traditional retirement stage of life is 59½ and older, the point when you can access your retirement accounts.

Once that stage of retirement is secure, you can attempt to finance an earlier retirement.

▶ Wherever possible, let your money accumulate in tax-sheltered accounts for as long as possible. It will grow faster. Use money in accounts that have already been taxed first.

≈ Laying the Groundwork for Early Retirement

I know what you're thinking. Here it comes. The lecture that if I want to retire early, I need to buy sacks of flour and start making my own bread. Or maybe, the advice will be to buy in bulk, like when Kramer on *Seinfeld* discovered the Price Club warehouse and bought 50 huge cans of Beef-a-reeno. He wound up feeding them to Rusty, a horse, but that's another story.

Unfortunately, saving money must be a part of every plan to retire early. But it's like listening to advice from your mother. It goes in one ear and out the other. And the next thing you know, you're old and still working and giving this same advice to kids who are rolling their eyes.

You may recall the garage sale episode of *Mad About You*. Cousin Ira brings cups of coffee to Paul and Jamie. Paul's mom is incredulous. With apologies to the TV viewers who are able to memorize dialogue, the conversation went something like this: "You bought coffee?" she asks with an astonished look on her face. "Who buys coffee? You make coffee."

Mrs. Buchman was every bit as surprised when visiting her son and his wife for Thanksgiving dinner. She and her husband were aghast that their son bought ice, instead of making it.

While you may be more like Paul and Jamie when it comes to saving money, there's a middle road that can lead you to early retirement. It starts by listening to advice about saving money and deciding if any of it is right for you. Try to avoid the knee-jerk negative reaction to money-saving advice.

One of my favorite financial experts is Humberto Cruz, who writes a column called "The Savings Game" for the *Sun-Sentinel*. In his column, he offers great tips on saving money. There are a few people, however, who react negatively to his advice. Cruz reports that one reader wrote a letter saying the columnist was off the deep end on the issue of saving. After Cruz told readers how he and his wife write down every penny they spend, the letter writer sarcastically commended Cruz's wife for sticking with him through 26 years of penny-pinching.

Continuing his sarcastic tone, the author of the letter expressed happiness that Cruz paid off his mortgage in three weeks and spent $1.59 on the family vacation. The letter writer claimed to have seen people saving every penny, only to get hit by a bus or stricken by cancer, and have their heirs spend the money over night.

Unfortunately, many people react to advice on saving money in this same way. The letter writer seemed to be saying that it's silly to save money because you might die and someone else will spend it. Therefore, you should blow the money.

Obviously, most responsible adults plan for the future. We spend money on life insurance, even though it won't do us any good after we're gone. We save for a rainy day, even though it would be much more fun to spend every penny we make. Saving for retirement, early or otherwise, will mean giving up things today. And that concept is repugnant to many people.

Saving for retirement does mean that you'll be reducing your living expenses and setting priorities. For us, cutting expenses didn't seem like a sacrifice. However, we also react negatively to penny-pinching that seems too drastic.

Financial expert Andrew Tobias has articulated the difference between frugal and cheap. Frugal is turning the lights off when you leave a room. Cheap is leaving a 10 percent tip. Frugal is avoiding hotels and motels with minibars. Cheap is buying your spouse something less nice than she'd like when you can easily afford to make her happy.

Cruz's wife and family don't seem too unhappy with him. They didn't spend $1.59 on a vacation as the letter writer suggested. On their 25th wedding anniversary, they celebrated by taking a two week trip to the Mediterranean along with their daughter and son-in-law. The trip cost Cruz $25,000, proving there are ways to save for retirement and still live a pretty nice life.

WHERE DO YOU STAND NOW?

Here's a little test. How much cash do you have in your wallet or purse? And how much did you spend yesterday or last week? Maybe you have no clue how much cash you spent or the amount outstanding on your credit card. For some people, their only concerns are having $15 per month to put toward the balance and not exceeding their credit limit. At the end of a weekend, can you estimate how many charges are on your credit card before adding up the receipts? Do you know how much is in your checking account?

Let's carry this premise a little further. Would you know your net worth off the top of your head? Do your assets exceed your liabilities? How much is in your 401(k) retirement savings account? If you have individual retirement accounts (IRAs), what rate of return are they getting?

Assuming you're not living payday to payday, it's easy to lose track of your assets. Years ago, I called the bank we deal with and was frantic. I was certain an IRA was missing. When I returned home and checked our records, I found it was lost at another bank. Though I had an idea how much the IRA was worth, I totally forgot that we opened it at a different financial institution.

When you're saving for long-term financial goals like retirement, it's easy to become complacent. If your retirement accounts are invested in certificates of deposit (CDs) at your bank, you'll get paperwork a few weeks prior to their maturity. If you ignore the paperwork, the CDs will automatically renew at the rate in effect at the time of renewal. Even though the rate of return is low, many of us never take the time to investigate other investment options. As a result, we'll wind up with thousands of dollars less in our retirement accounts, because we're too busy to be bothered.

If you're giving any thought at all to retiring early, you must find out where you stand now. The first step is making a list of every asset you have, as well as every debt you owe. Write down every asset you own, whether it's your house, car, or stamp collection. Try to be realistic in your appraisal of their worth. The chart below should be helpful.

Net Worth

Primary Residence (fair market value less mortgage)	$ _____
Vacation Home and Other Real Estate (fair market value less mortgage)	$ _____
401(k) or Other Retirement Plans	$ _____
IRAs	$ _____
Bank Accounts	$ _____
Mutual Funds	$ _____
Stocks	$ _____
Other Investments	$ _____
Collectibles, Misc. Personal Property	$ _____
Automobiles (fair market value less loan)	$ _____
Subtotal	$ _____
Subtract Other Debts (loans, credit cards, college debt)	$ _____
Grand (or not so grand) Total	$ _____

For the next month, write down every expenditure from a major purchase on your credit card to the bagel you buy from the guy who comes every morning to your office at 9:00. Not many people like the idea of writing down every penny they spend. While it's not something you want to do all the time, it's a very good place to start. It's an essential step in getting a handle on your finances. You need to know how much you earn and spend. You really need to track your spending for at least a month or longer. Look back over the past six months to determine how much you saved and spent. It won't be as accurate as your detailed account of this month, but you'll start to see a pattern.

The act of writing down expenditures helps you determine where the leaks in your budget are. The few bucks here and there add up to big dollars. It's much like a small water leak that can make a big difference in your water bill. By keeping track of the money you spend, you're exercising control over your money, not penny-pinching.

As you go through your expenditures, you need to question whether you might have lived without them. Maybe that great $35 tie has already been relegated to the second string or never gets worn any more because your company has moved toward casual clothes. Perhaps, those too-good-to-pass-up shoes hurt your bunion and weren't the bargain you thought they'd be.

There may have even been major purchases that were a disappointment. For one couple, the trip to Puerto Rico was a letdown. Their plane sat on the runway at JFK for two hours and didn't arrive at their destination until 1:00 AM Saturday morning. For $2,000 each, they got three days of nice weather and two rounds of golf. They never made it to the rain forest because of their concern about dengue fever. And to top it off, the limo driver wasn't waiting on their return because their plane circled the airport for 45 minutes.

Maybe, you took a vacation at a spa that didn't meet your expectations. Or maybe you flew 12 hours for a Hawaiian vacation to escape the hectic pace at work, only to find the same problems awaiting you on your return.

If you're seeking a lifestyle change, rather than an escape, these are issues you must address. When the choice comes down to watching the clock while you're waiting for quitting time or watching your spending so you can retire early, the decision is a little easier.

WHERE DO YOU WANT TO BE?

Even as you save for early retirement, you should still be able to live nicely now. The goal of the advice you'll read in this book is for you to strike a balance between living the good life now and planning for the future. Planning for the day when work ends doesn't mean giving up everything now. Though you're saving for the future, you can still enjoy yourself today.

The initial step is to prioritize your goals. Perhaps, your goal is to retire early, but you also want to build a swimming pool, or cement pond as the Clampetts used to say on *The Beverly Hillbillies*. There is no escaping the fact that expenditures like this may extend the amount of time you must spend in the workforce. If early retirement is your top priority, you may want to forgo the pool.

In some instances, you can have it all. For example, if you plan to sell your house at a profit to help finance your early retirement, the money put into the pool may be recouped to a certain extent. Real estate agents can tell you which home improvements add to the resale value of a house in your area and if you can expect a dollar-for-dollar return on your money. More likely than not, you won't get back the money you spend on a pool. Therefore, you're back to the threshold question: Is retiring early more important than enjoying a swimming pool in the backyard right now?

Every day, all of us set priorities regarding how we spend money. The makeup man for a television series asked the host what his indulgences were. The host indicated that he was always willing to spend money on clothes. On the other hand, the makeup man drove a much nicer car than the host, even though the host made a great deal more money.

All of us spend money on what we view to be important. Some people give a lot more money to charity than others, even though they make much less. To some people, owning a nice house is much more important than taking a lavish vacation. There are some people who make very little money but lavish gifts on others. That's important to them and it makes them feel good.

Once again, the purpose of this book isn't to make you change your priorities. Only you can determine your priorities and their importance. But you must realize that if you hope to reach the goal of early retirement, your priorities may have to change. For my wife and me, our top priority was to be financially independent and free to chuck our jobs if we desired.

One of my wife's former coworkers was always making jabs about our lifestyle. He knew we pulled in a pretty good buck, yet drove a modest car. The guy couldn't understand that we were reluctant to buy depreciating assets like an automobile and inclined to buy appreciating assets such as a house. For some reason, it bothered him that my wife and I shopped at Sym's and T.J. Maxx, not Sak's Fifth Avenue and Bloomingdale's.

He was really annoyed that we used the Entertainment book, which offers discounts on dining and travel. Frequently, he'd snidely ask where we were going with our coupon book that evening. Often, it was a nice restaurant that used discounts to attract diners on a night when most people didn't eat out. The coworker never quite got it that we were happy with our lifestyle. We didn't feel we were giving up anything.

My wife and I are not high-maintenance people. We're not into impulse spending. But I don't think we're obsessive about compulsive saving either, though my wife's coworker would disagree. Our philosophy is that before buying something, you make sure it's something you truly want and then shop around for the best price.

Saving money comes easier to some than it does to others. Some people think nothing about paying $6 for slice of cheesecake to die for, while others would rather die than spend $6 for a slice of cheesecake. Some people can't imagine dinner out without drinks and an expensive bottle of wine, while that's not important to others. Depending on your mind-set, saving is going to be very easy or very difficult.

Ask yourself if most of your dinners out are memorable, aside from the charge on your credit card statement. Or maybe you spend $8 for a movie every Saturday night, yet you only enjoyed a few of them. If you can't wait for movies to come out on video, you might at least hold off until they hit the bargain theaters.

Perhaps, you're the type who buys a top-of-the-line computer, even though you use only a few of the features. While other people were buying computers for $3,000, we bought a used one for a few hundred dollars. It met our needs for a long time. We can now get a bigger and better one for about $1000, including the monitor and a decent printer. It took no stroke of genius on our part, just patience and careful shopping.

Obviously, it doesn't pay to buy some things used. With 25-inch television sets hovering around the $200 mark, buying used would be foolish. And when buying clothing, some people swear by consignment shops, while others get the best deal they can on new clothes. Just don't spend your retirement watching TV and shopping for clothes.

HONEY, I SHRUNK THE BUDGET

As I mentioned in Chapter 1, your spouse or significant other must share your priorities. If the special person in your life believes you're off the deep end when it comes to saving money, your relationship might head off the deep end.

One of the biggest expenditures in your budget is your house. When I talk more about a strategy for early retirement, I'll discuss a number of options for cutting housing costs. The best way to enter the early retirement stage of your life is with a paid-off mortgage. Although financial planners will tell you about the tax advantages of having a large mortgage, there's at least one big reason why you should pay it off and it's a psychological one. You're going to feel an enormous sense of freedom when it's paid off. But while it may be a terrific feeling, taking your ready cash and paying off the mortgage isn't necessarily the quick road to early retirement. In fact, if you cut yourself short by paying off your mortgage, you may find yourself delaying retirement until your ready cash is replenished.

In Chapter 11, I'll talk about options such as taking advantage of the new tax break on the sale of your primary residence. By selling your house, you may be able to collect enough funds to sustain your lifestyle until you're eligible to draw from retirement accounts or your pension.

If you can't bear to part with a house that holds so many memories, another option is renting it. Assuming you can rent it for more than its monthly expenses, you'll pick up a little extra cash. The down side is you'll need to live elsewhere, but if you own a vacation home, this may fit perfectly into your plans. In Chapter 11, we'll look at these issues in depth.

For now, our only concern is cutting your expenses. For many people, a monthly mortgage payment takes the biggest chunk out of their paycheck. When you add taxes, utilities, upkeep, maintenance, and other expenses, the cost is even more significant. Selling a home that's too big for you can lead to a sizable reduction in the money necessary to maintain your lifestyle.

Another big-ticket item in a typical family's lifestyle is the family auto, autos, or fleet of autos. To retire early, you might have to give up the luxury car. However, everyone needs a dependable car even if you aren't going off to work each day. Ideally, you'll have a relatively new and dependable car to take into retirement with you.

Leasing can save you cash, but it's not necessarily the long-term solution. Instead of eventually owning a car that will last years longer because you're driving it less, you'll be faced with a new lease every few years. Psychologically and financially, you'll be better off not having to go out and get a new car until you're fully adjusted to life in retirement.

Once again, cutting expenses in this area (or any area for that matter) won't sit well with everyone. Therefore, I'll repeat a theme of this book that you'll eventually be sick of hearing. Early retirement isn't for everyone. If this is a sacrifice you don't want to make, don't make it and don't retire early. No one is forcing you to set different priorities. You can still retire early and drive a nice car. It just might not be a Lexus.

In March of 1998, the general manager of a Rolls Royce dealership offered his rationale for driving a Rolls. He said that the buyer of a Rolls is generally wealthier than the buyer of other luxury cars like Mercedes-Benz, Jaguar, or Cadillac. He even suggested a lease arrangement at a price of $500 to $600 per month. According to the general manager, a customer can be assured that he's in an elite class and will never see his bartender at a red light driving the same car. If you aspire to drive a luxury car, you should question whether your ulterior motive is to be in some elite class. If so, you could forgo the luxury car and be in an elite class of people who are retiring early.

A major step to controlling expenses is making a budget and sticking to it. One woman found that she and her husband were going to the automated teller machine too often. They started an envelope system for tracking their cash. The couple budgeted a specified amount for entertainment, baby-sitting, gas, and household expenses. Every week, they put the appropriate amount of cash to cover each expense in a separate envelope. When the cash in an envelope gets low, they know it's time to cut back in that area. If there's no cash left in the entertainment envelope, they won't eat out or go to a movie.

If a system works for someone, you really shouldn't quibble with it. Many people, however, won't have the discipline to stick to this system. When they run out of cash, they'll pay for dinner with a credit card.

In every budget, unexpected expenditures will arise. Conversely, you *find* money periodically. On a business trip, your meals are paid for or you get a per diem to cover them. Or perhaps, a lunch is on the company expense account or provided by the boss for a noontime meeting. In these instances, the key is making certain the money you didn't have to spend doesn't slip through your fingers. The amounts are small, but they can make a difference in the long run.

At a going-away lunch for a colleague, everyone in our office brought in tons of great food. There was enough left over for everyone to eat well for several days afterwards. An hour before the going-away lunch, a group of programmers went out to McDonald's for a pre-lunch snack. While one of them may become the next Bill Gates, their food budgets might have benefited from skipping that particular meal.

One member of that group used to buy four *supersized* soft drinks from McDonald's each day. Even at inexpensive restaurants like McDonald's, small expenditures add up quickly. I am not suggesting that you give up these small pleasures that eat away at your budget. These are simply areas where you might consider cutting corners. Another way to shave your dining out budget would be to replace a meal at a waterfront restaurant with a picnic on the beach.

Of course, sometimes eating out can be cheaper than staying home to cook. At a Taco Bell in south Florida, seniors get free beverages with any purchase. For some, dinner is two 69 cent tacos. On other days, people of any age can have 29 cent hamburgers at McDonald's. And there's a pizza place that offers all-you-can-eat pizza and salad for $2.99. But if you plan to live a long time in retirement, those eating habits aren't going to help.

Before you eat another Big Mac, take a look at what you're spending now and how much you expect to spend in retirement.

Monthly Expenses	Current	Retirement
Mortgage or Rent	_____	_____
Property Taxes	_____	_____
Home-Related Expenses (upkeep, maintenance fees)	_____	_____
Utilities	_____	_____
Auto-Related Expenses (loans, lease, gas, tolls, repairs)	_____	_____
Food	_____	_____
Clothing	_____	_____

Insurance (health, life, auto)   _____   _____

Medical Expenses   _____   _____

Personal Care   _____   _____

Entertainment   _____   _____

Travel   _____   _____

Loan Payments   _____   _____
(credit cards, home equity, school)

Miscellaneous   _____   _____

Total   _____   _____

GETTING MORE OUT OF LIFE FOR LESS

Robert Otterbourg, author of *Retire and Thrive,* tells a story about two retirees who wanted to visit Europe. One went first class, staying at the finest hotels, while the other took advantage of Elder Hostels, an inexpensive lodging alternative for senior citizens. When all was said and done, both saw Europe. One did it, however, for far less money.

To stick to a budget for a long period of time, it's imperative that you don't feel you're making sacrifices. You're simply making concessions in your lifestyle. It's not a question of living for today versus living for tomorrow; it's living for 3,650 tomorrows if you retire ten years early.

Let's take a small example like gourmet coffee. While I love coffee, I have difficulty spending a few bucks for a cup. I honestly can't tell the difference between a good cup of coffee and the premium kind. Sometimes, I wonder if others can either. I get more compliments when I add vanilla to a pot of store brand coffee than when I brew the premium brand. Nevertheless, if you feel gourmet coffee adds something to your life, don't subtract it from your budget.

If you're young enough, the smallest budget cut can bring big returns down the road. If you're 25, $5 a day or $100 per month compounds to $800,000 at age 65. And that's assuming just a normal rate of return, not a great rate of return. If you can't cut the coffee budget, then maybe your phone bill where you can either call less or get a better rate. Maybe, you can cut out some of those services (that I hate) like call waiting. Do it for me, if not yourself.

Even if you're a lot older than 25, small cuts in your budget, if invested properly, can produce great long-term returns. I'm not saying don't eat out, but maybe you can give up an expensive appetizer or a pricey dessert. Who knows? It might lead to saving money and losing weight.

Shifting your paradigms can help you get more out of life for less. You've probably heard so much about shifting paradigms at work, it's made you want to retire early. But it can save you money. At a five-star restaurant in Boca Raton, Florida, there is a less expensive fixed price menu available every day but Saturday. When we eat there on a special occasion, we don't go on a Saturday, which should come as no surprise by now.

In a *Seinfeld* episode, Jerry's father is accused by his condo association of embezzling funds, because they catch him eating a regular price dinner instead of the early bird special. Early birds don't necessarily equal early retirement, but they're one way to save if you can stomach them. Shifting paradigms may mean eating earlier, if your schedule permits and a restaurant offers specials for dining before a certain time. It's probably healthier too. Eating lunch at a better restaurant will be easier on the wallet than having dinner there.

In some areas, shifting your grocery shopping days will get you additional discounts on merchandise. Publix Supermarket in Florida frequently offers several dollars off your order for shopping on Monday. Maybe by switching brands you can cut your grocery costs. On the other hand, don't buy fattening foods simply because they're less expensive.

By shifting your paradigms, you can enjoy the same activities for less money. Vacations when it's not peak season can save you money. If you must go to Paris in the springtime or prime vacation season, plan on spending *beaucoup* dollars. Similarly, a trip to Wildwood, New Jersey, costs far less in June or September than July or August.

With some activities, it's tough to shift your paradigms. It's usually cheaper to play golf during the week instead of the weekend, but your boss may not look favorably on this plan. On a sports talk show recently, callers were offering tips on the best golf values in the area. Instead of paying $100 for 18 holes and a golf cart, callers found terrific courses for as little as $18, including the golf cart, although weekends cost $8 more.

You may, however, feel like Kramer did in one episode of *Seinfeld*. He traded Cuban cigars for rounds of golf at a country club. After playing country club courses, Kramer couldn't bear the thought of going back to the public courses. If club memberships are a part of your lifestyle that you're not willing to forgo, your budget can't be cut in that area. In an online question-and-answer session, one financial planner said he underestimated his client's expenses of $25,000 per year on golf-related activities.

Once again, whether it's an Entertainment coupon book or some other discount card, you can often find reduced rates on recreational activities. However, using coupons is not an acceptable practice for some people. When we were getting an oil change recently at a Jiffy Lube franchise, we saw people paying full price despite the fact that the company bombards residents in the area with coupons.

Car repairs can also put an unexpected dent in your budget unless your car is under warranty. But saving money doesn't mean you should avoid preventive maintenance. It may, however, mean washing and detailing the car yourself.

And cars aren't the only things that are expensive to maintain, even with coupons. Some people have expensive toys that make it tough for them to retire early. If you own a boat, you're already aware of the expense. Cruising up and down the water every day isn't cheap. You'll need to budget accordingly if boating is what you plan to do in retirement.

Other people have high-priced recreational toys like jet skis. I recently saw a recreational watercraft on sale for $6,000, reduced from $7,500. And don't forget the upkeep and fuel. You'd be better off buying yourself a kayak.

Beach communities are filled with people engaging in free activities that require a relatively small investment. They're throwing Frisbees. They're skating on the roadway by the water. They're bicycling through parks. In almost every community, people can shoot baskets or play tennis on public courts.

Recreational activities won't necessarily break your budget. Necessities can do the most damage at the wrong time, like sitting on your glasses or losing them. I must prefer sitting on them, because I do it frequently. The key is to budget for these inevitable problems and get the best deal you can on your purchase.

A woman bought a pair of prescription glasses and was shocked when she picked them up. She was charged $600, which included an eye exam. The woman never asked what the final charge would be. She simply agreed to every extra offered by the person selling the glasses. As hard as it is to believe, there are some people who don't ask prices in advance, and there are others who don't blink at several hundred dollars for nonprescription sunglasses.

There are things that some people aren't willing to give up, even if it will help them retire earlier. That's fine as long as it's a conscious decision and you realize you'll need to save more cash for retirement and you may need to make bigger cuts in some other area of your budget.

HOW MUCH DO I NEED?

At last count, Bill Gates' net worth jumped to $51 billion. One might assume that Bill has enough to retire, should his antitrust problems become too aggravating. The more important issue is whether *you* have enough to retire.

According to the old song "Spinning Wheel," what goes up, must come down. Most financial planners believe that's the case in retirement. Instead of going up, your budget usually comes down. The rule of thumb is that you'll need 70 to 80 percent of your current salary per year to live on during retirement.

The basis for that rule of thumb is that your needs are less when you're out of the workforce. You'll be able to avoid commuting expenses and lunches out. Your wardrobe expenses should go down, unless you're planning to shop for clothes every day. Ideally, you'll be spending the day in a bathing suit and won't need much more in the way of clothes.

The trouble with any rule of thumb is that it can't be relied on, and by using it you may make some incorrect assumptions about your lifestyle. One basic problem is that it presumes you're living on every penny of your salary now which you really shouldn't be. Many two-income families live on one salary and bank the other. Some scale back their lifestyle, so that one of the spouses can quit and stay home with the kids.

If two spouses make $50,000 each, the income of the household is $100,000 per year. That doesn't necessarily mean that they will need 80 percent or $80,000 per year in retirement. A better rule of thumb would be 80 percent of the income on which you could comfortably live now. If that's $60,000, you would need about $48,000. The sooner you find out what your actual needs are, the sooner you'll find out what you'll need in retirement. You'll also determine what you should be saving.

The American Savings Education Council has prepared a terrific worksheet to help you estimate how much savings you'll need when you retire. Unlike most worksheets, it doesn't require a lot of math, just a few minutes of your time. You can use the rule of thumb the council suggests as a starting point or plug in the actual amount of income you think you'll need.

The chart gives you a general idea of how much to save each year. Whatever the amount, start saving and investing today. You'll have $100,000 in 30 years, just by saving $120 per month with a 5 percent after-tax rate of return. If you procrastinate and try to accumulate $100,000 in 10 years, you'll need to save $641 per month. The small amounts that you save now will compound and grow quickly over the years.

At a minimum, you should be saving 10 percent of your income. If you can't, you're either overextended or lack discipline. Many financial planners advocate the 80/20 rule. Use 80 percent of your earnings for living expenses and save 20 per-

BALLPARK E$TIMATE™

Planning for retirement is not a one-size-fits-all exercise. The purpose of Ballpark is simply to give you a basic idea of the savings you'll need when you retire. *So let's play ball!*

1. How much annual income will you want in retirement? (Figure 70% of your current annual gross income just to maintain your current standard of living. Really.) $ _____

2. Subtract the income you expect to receive annually from:
   - Social Security—If you make under $25,000, enter $8,000; between $25,000 - $40,000, enter $12,000; over $40,000, enter $14,500 -$ _____
   - Traditional Employer Pension - a plan that pays a set dollar amount for life, where the dollar amount depends on salary and years of service (in today's dollars) -$ _____
   - Part-time income -$ _____
   - Other -$ _____

   This is how much you need to make up for each retirement year: =$ _____

   Now you want a ballpark estimate of how much money you'll need in the bank the day you retire. So the accountants went to work and devised this simple formula. For the record, they figure you'll realize a constant real rate of return of 3% after inflation, you'll live to age 87, and you'll begin to receive income from Social Security at age 65.

3. To determine the amount you'll need to save, multiply the amount you need to make up by the factor below. $ _____

Age you expect to retire:		Your factor is:	
	55		21.0
	60		18.9
	65		16.4
	70		13.6

4. If you expect to retire before age 65, multiply your Social Security benefit from line 2 by the factor below. +$ _____

Age you expect to retire:		Your factor is:	
	55		8.8
	60		4.7

5. Multiply your savings to date by the factor below (include money accumulated in a 401(k), IRA, or similar retirement plan). -$ _____

If you want to retire in:		Your factor is:	
	10 years		1.3
	15 years		1.6
	20 years		1.8
	25 years		2.1
	30 years		2.4
	35 years		2.8
	40 years		3.3

   Total additional savings needed at retirement: =$ _____

   Don't panic. Those same accountants devised another formula to show you how much to save each year in order to reach your goal amount. They factor in compounding. That's where your money not only makes interest, your interest starts making interest as well, creating a snowball effect.

6. To determine the ANNUAL amount you'll need to save, multiply the TOTAL amount by the factor below. =$ _____

If you want to retire in:		Your factor is:	
	10 years		.085
	15 years		.052
	20 years		.036
	25 years		.027
	30 years		.020
	35 years		.016
	40 years		.013

ASEC
AMERICAN SAVINGS EDUCATION COUNCIL™

ASEC/EBRI-ERF
Suite 600
2121 K Street NW
Washington, DC
20037-1896
202-775-9130 or
202-659-0670
Fax 202-775-6312
www.asec.org
www.ebri.org

See? It's not impossible or even particularly painful. It just takes planning. And the sooner you start, the better off you'll be.

This worksheet simplifies several retirement planning issues such as projected Social Security benefits and earnings assumptions on savings. It also reflects today's dollars; therefore you will need to re-calculate your retirement needs annually and as your salary and circumstances change. You may want to consider doing further analysis, either by yourself using a more detailed worksheet or computer software or with the assistance of a financial professional. 1/98

cent. Target 10 percent now and increase the amount you're saving after you become accustomed to living on less.

Wherever possible, use savings vehicles that are deducted from your paycheck. You aren't tempted to spend that money because it's invested before you get your hands on it. You're paying yourself first instead of saving from what's left in your paycheck.

Though the general rule is that you'll need less to live on in retirement, some of those savings will be offset by inflation. If you retire at age 55, you may be going 30 years or longer without a paycheck. You won't have a salary going up each year to meet the rising cost of living. According to the American Society of Chartered Life Underwriters and Chartered Financial Consultants, if inflation runs at 4 percent, it will take $155,933 in 30 years to equal the purchasing power that $50,000 has today.

Because you're planning for the pre–59½ stage of retirement, as well as the post–59½ stage, inflation will be less of a problem. The money set aside for after age 59½ will be invested in mutual funds that should keep up with inflation. By avoiding conservative investments, the funds set aside for the period prior to age 59½ will also keep pace with inflation. In addition, your budget should always be higher than what you'll actually need to live on, so there's room for unexpected expenses and prices that escalate because of inflation.

To retire before age 59½, you need to create that pool of ready cash. If you need $50,000 per year to live on, every $50,000 you save that isn't tied up in a tax-sheltered account represents a year sooner you can retire. If you build the account to $100,000, that's two years sooner. You're working backwards from the magic date of 59½, using the funds you can access before that date. However, make certain that you've fully prepared for the post–59½ stage of your life.

Rules of the Road to Early Retirement

▶ Saving for early retirement involves setting priorities. To increase the amount you're saving, you may need to make cuts elsewhere in your budget.

▶ Make no major purchases without sleeping on it for a few days and consulting *Consumer Reports* or researching what you're buying.

▶ Alright already with the impulse buying. Learn how to walk the mall without buying anything. Work at being a saver instead of a consumer.

▶ Count your cash before you go to work every day. See what's left that evening and figure out where it went. Track your spending for a month and see where the leaks are.

▶ Shoot to save 20 percent of your paycheck. Wherever possible, sign up for investments like 401(k) retirement savings plans that are deducted before you get your hands on the money.

≈ Investing for Retirement

In an editorial cartoon, aging baby boomers grieve over the loss of their childhood favorites. The wife mourns the loss of Roy Rogers, Robert Young from *Father Knows Best,* Buffalo Bob, and Shari Lewis and Lamb Chop. She asks, "What does it all mean?" Her husband replies, "Maybe we should start thinking about saving for our retirement."

About time. Whether you're a baby boomer or a member of Generation X, you'll never get to retire early just by saving money. You need to invest it as well. Savings are funds you set aside from your income. Investing is the act of making your savings grow.

To retire early, you'll need to do more with your money than just put it in a savings account. To appreciate how important it is to seek a higher rate of return on your money, it is useful to look at the rule of 72. The rule of 72 allows you to calculate how long it takes for your money to double. Divide 72 by the rate of return you're getting. If you make a 6 percent return on your money, your funds will double in 12 years. 72 divided by 6 equals 12.

Hopefully, you don't need a calculator to utilize the rule of 72. If you can get an 8 percent rate of return, your money will double in 9 years. An additional 1 percent rate of return will enable you to double your money in 8 years. 72 divided by 9 is 8.

Obviously, if you can get a higher rate of return, your money will double more quickly. A 12 percent rate of return will double your money in 6 years. Along with a greater rate of return comes the element of risk. Your money may not double at all. In fact, your principal may decrease.

So how do you increase your rate of return without losing ground? In a "Dilbert" cartoon, Dogbert is getting financial advice. A man holding a lengthy document tells him, "We can handle your investments so you can retire and live off the earnings. Just sign this incomprehensible contract, hand all your money to total strangers and relax!". In the final frame of the cartoon, he says, "We'll need to know what your tolerance to risk is." Dogbert replies, "I think I just maxed out."

Although you probably don't earn as much as Scott Adams, the creator of "Dilbert," you work hard for your money. While everyone dreams of watching their money make money, there is a certain amount of risk when you invest.

Right from the get-go, you need to analyze your investment temperament. Some people are comfortable with risky investments, while others will lose sleep over losing even a small amount of money. Those with a low threshold for risk will watch the value of their investments fluctuate each day and will agonize over small losses, even if they're only on paper. Therefore, your portfolio should be structured with your tolerance for risk in mind.

Some people will need to invest aggressively to retire early. If they're getting a late start on saving for retirement, they have to catch up and can't depend upon conservative investments. It's not a strategy recommended for those averse to risk.

Investors with little tolerance for risk probably aren't aware that they are subject to different forms of risk with their safer investments. They risk a loss in purchasing power, if their investments don't keep up with inflation. They also risk interest rates falling on their supposedly safe investment. Even though their principal doesn't erode, the lack of growth is a risk they aren't considering.

Equity investments like stock scare a lot of people. They watch the newspaper every day and can't deal with any drops in value. Investors with little tolerance for risk don't realize there are ways to couch their bets and minimize the risk they're facing. Diversifying your assets is the best way to reduce your risk. You're spreading your money around, so your fortunes aren't tied to one type of investment.

Investing for the long haul also minimizes your risk. You don't worry about short-term fluctuations in the value of your investments and bank on the long-term growth of the market. By maintaining an emergency fund, you won't have to liquidate your long-term investments at the wrong time to get cash.

In addition, there are equity investments that are less risky. Conservative equity funds like large-cap value funds are less volatile than other investments in the stock market. These funds invest in large companies that appear to be undervalued. A stock index mutual fund is also less risky. These mutual funds are tied to a stock index such as Standard & Poor's 500.

On the other hand, certain equity investments are more risky. Emerging markets funds look for stocks in countries with new, small, or developing stock markets. They are extremely volatile. Small company funds typically invest in stocks traded "over the counter." Because they are particularly susceptible to business setbacks, their price volatility is high. Precious metal funds are also extremely risky. High-risk investments don't always result in higher rates of return, even if you stick with them for a long time.

TURNING TO THE MONEY EXPERTS

Like Dogbert, you can hire someone to manage your money. For purposes of this book, we'll assume you don't just turn money over to someone to invest. However, the services of a financial planner can help most people determine if they are on course to the goal of early retirement or whatever objective they're trying to achieve.

A fee-based financial planner is generally the best choice. For a flat fee, the planner will help you chart the course toward your financial objectives. The fee won't be cheap, however. It might be in the neighborhood of $5,000 for a comprehensive plan, plus charges for annual updates. Fee-based planners do not make a commission on the products they recommend, so their advice is more objective than someone who will benefit from the sale of products recommended.

The selection of a financial planner shouldn't be made on the basis of fees. If someone charges too small an amount, that person may actually be making money on the products recommended. Every year *Worth* magazine selects the best financial planners in America. While its selection process is hardly foolproof, it might give you the name of someone in your area to consider.

The operative word is *consider.* When choosing a financial planner, you should consider more than one. Ask for recommendations from friends, relatives, and colleagues. Find out the planner's fees in advance and how long the planning process will take. Fee-only planners are going to be more expensive than those who earn commissions from the products they recommend.

Financial planners who make their living on fees only usually belong to an organization called The National Association of Personal Financial Advisors. The organization can supply the names of fee-only planners in your area. The organization can be reached at 888-FEE-ONLY (888-333-6659). The organization's Web site can be found at www.napfa.org.

Just as you wouldn't choose a physician without an M.D. after his or her name, you should look for financial planners with credentials. The most important designation for an adviser is CFP, which stands for Certified Financial Planner. Certified Financial Planners must meet rigid standards. They are required to take ten courses and must have spent a designated amount of time counseling clients. They also must comply with continuing education requirements. The Institute of Certified

Financial Planners will give you the names of CFPs who practice in your area to help you avoid encountering someone who claims to have the designation but really doesn't. The Institute of Certified Financial Planners can be reached at 800-282-PLAN (800-282-7526). The organization's Web site can be located at www.icfp.org.

A relatively new designation is CPA/PFS. It is the designation for Certified Public Accountants (CPAs) who have expertise in financial planning. CPAs who have earned the Personal Financial Specialist (PFS) designation have passed a comprehensive exam covering all areas of financial planning and possess extensive experience in the field. The American Institute of Certified Public Accountants' Web site can be found at www.aicpa.org. The organization will not, however, recommend CPAs. Although the national organization won't make referrals, a statewide group might provide this information.

The Registered Investment Advisor (RIA) designation beside someone's name means that person has registered with the Securities and Exchange Commission (SEC). It doesn't necessarily mean that the person has special training in personal finance.

Chartered Financial Consultant (ChFC) and Chartered Life Underwriter (CLU) are designations awarded by the American College in Bryn Mawr, Pennsylvania. The ChFC designation is conferred for meeting requirements and passing exams in the financial planning area. The CLU designation is awarded for expertise in insurance-related areas. Traditionally, individuals with these designations have a background in the insurance industry.

Many people like to call themselves financial advisers, but don't necessarily have the credentials to offer comprehensive advice on personal finance. Bankers, insurance agents, and stockbrokers may be more interested in selling their particular products than looking at the big financial picture. Insurance agents may be pushing life insurance products to meet your needs in retirement, even though some other investment might be more appropriate. With life insurance products, the commission might be as much as 100 percent of the first year premium and less in subsequent years.

A survey commissioned by the American Association of Retired Persons (AARP) indicates that older investors have a limited understanding of how brokers are compensated. Though they know that brokers are paid commissions, there are serious gaps in their understanding of the broker compensation system. Women age 50 and older have a particular problem understanding the system.

The study found that only about one in three older investors knows that higher-risk investments often involve higher commissions for the brokers selling them. More than one-third did not know that their initial investment is reduced by the *load*, which is the sales charge. Almost half the people surveyed did not realize a broker's commission is negotiable. One-third did not realize that some firms use contests to promote the sale of a particular investment product.

The AARP offers a number of tips to investors dealing with brokers and advises to ask for full disclosure of all investment costs such as commissions. Be wary of brokers who may be participating in a contest for selling certain products. These contests and bonuses are likely to influence the broker's recommendations.

Learn how to read your brokerage account statements. And if the fees you're paying are too steep and the advice from your broker is suspect, use a discount broker. Discount brokerage firms can cut the cost of each financial transaction.

Before dealing with any broker, or any financial professional for that matter, check out the person's disciplinary record through the National Association of Securities Dealers (NASD). The public disclosure line can be reached by calling 800-289-9999. The Web site for the NASD is www.nasd.com. You can also contact the state securities regulator in your state to see if additional information is available. Always be certain a broker is properly registered to do business in your state.

Ask to see a copy of both parts of Form ADV, the materials that most financial advisers file with the SEC. Part One of Form ADV provides detailed information about the adviser's past. It will note any disciplinary action taken against him or her. Part Two provides extensive information on the adviser's education, industry affiliations, and the services offered. If the adviser is reluctant to provide both parts of Form ADV, head for the door.

If you want to do it yourself, you can use personal finance software like Quicken or Microsoft Money. These programs provide numerous money management tools. If you use them, it's easy to take stock of your assets and liabilities. You'll see how the rate of return affects the amount you'll accumulate over the years. A greater rate of return, even 1 or 2 percent, can make a huge difference in how quickly your money will grow.

The Quicken Web site also provides a wealth of investment information. It is located at www.quicken.com. The Microsoft Money Web site can be found at www.microsoft.com/money.

YOU CAN GO YOUR OWN WAY

If you're the self-reliant type and don't want to engage the services of a financial planner, there are many good and bad ways to get advice about investing. One bad way is to listen to radio investment programs where the host pays for air time. Often, these hosts tout stocks they are being paid to promote. Listeners believe they are hearing objective advice, but the programs are basically infomercials. The host pays anywhere from $100 to $2,000 per hour for airtime on the station.

State regulators, as well as the SEC, have filed numerous civil complaints against people who fail to disclose that they're being paid to tout a stock. The Manhattan U.S. Attorney, Mary Jo White, is quoted as saying that radio and television enhance the credibility of the advice. But without full disclosure, listeners are being misled.

There are radio talk shows that do provide objective advice. The worst criticism that might be leveled against them is that they're as dry as anything you've ever heard and the host is anxious for listeners to become clients. The advice is often for the caller to stop by the office for a more thorough explanation of the answer to his or her question.

Personal finance fairs are usually a good way to learn about investing, unless the sponsor is a group pushing a particular investment product. Local chapters of the International Association for Financial Planning sponsor fairs across the country. The guests are usually personal finance columnists and noted experts on investing, not salespeople. The International Association for Financial Planning's Web site can be found at www.iafp.org. The organization's phone number is 404-845-0011.

In contrast, there are often *seminars* conducted at local hotels, offering free meals and information. Too many times the information is slanted, so you'll buy a particular investment that *coincidentally* the instructor markets. A better choice is a class offered at your local high school or college. Often, the classes are taught by stockbrokers or financial advisers, so the advice won't be totally unbiased. The tuition is usually a charge of the university, not the instructor who normally teaches for free to generate business.

The Internet is a wonderful tool for learning about investments. There is a great deal of information out there that can be extremely useful. Always remember, however, that the information may be tainted. The person putting the information on the Internet may have a particular bias or a product to sell. Many Internet sites are not created as a public service but are commercial in nature.

TYPES OF MUTUAL FUNDS

Mutual funds make it easy to go your own way. Funds are professionally managed by experts who spend their day analyzing stocks and other investment products. With a mutual fund, an amateur investor stands a much better chance of achieving financial independence.

There are many different types of mutual funds with diverse investment objectives. Morningstar, Chicago-based independent mutual fund rating and analysis service, separates mutual funds into these four groups:

1. Domestic equity funds (U.S. stocks)
2. International equity funds (international stocks)
3. Taxable bond funds (U.S. and international bonds)
4. Municipal bond funds

Although there are many different types of funds, Morningstar uses these categories as part of its ranking system. Morningstar's toll-free number is 800-735-0700, and its Web address is www.morningstar.net.

The Wall Street Journal divides mutual funds into four broad categories. They are stock funds, taxable bond funds, municipal bond funds, and stock and bond funds. Within those broad categories, the funds are divided into classifications by Lipper, Inc. Lipper publishes performance data and rankings for each classification. See www.lipperweb.com.

Basically, your choice is between aggressive, moderate, and conservative mutual funds. A conservative fund has low volatility, which means there's little turnover in its portfolio. Therefore, you're not likely to see huge upswings in the value of the fund. The flip side is that you're unlikely to lose your shirt on the investment.

A mutual fund company will offer dozens of mutual funds with different investment objectives. For example, equity income funds invest in stocks with a healthy dividend. A secondary objective is capital appreciation, which simply means that the price of the stock will hopefully increase. Although they focus on dividend-paying stocks, equity income funds may own some government and corporate bonds. They are sometimes called income stock funds.

Growth-and-income funds are a little different. These funds invest in stocks that are expected to grow significantly over the long haul and also seek income.

Growth funds are a little more risky. The managers of these funds hope to buy stocks that will increase in value. They are less concerned with whether these stocks pay dividends.

International funds invest in companies that do business overseas. These funds are riskier than those that invest in companies doing business in the United States.

Balanced funds invest in a mix of bonds, preferred stock, and common stock. The goal is to blend stocks that will grow in value with securities that pay income from dividends. At least one-quarter of the money is invested in bonds. Balanced funds are less risky than growth funds.

Income funds seek, guess what, income. These types of funds invest mostly in bonds. Short-term bond funds invest in bonds with a maturity of one to three years. These income funds generally pay a higher rate of interest than a money market fund, but the risk is slightly greater.

Money market funds invest in short-term securities. They are not insured by the government. They're extremely liquid and are a good parking spot for funds you'll need soon for an emergency or some particular purpose. It's extremely rare to lose money in a money market fund but not impossible. Don't confuse this type of fund with a money market deposit account, which is a bank account that is insured by the federal government.

GETTING INFORMATION ABOUT MUTUAL FUNDS

You can find a great deal of information about mutual funds on the Internet. Many mutual fund companies have established Web sites that provide important facts about their funds. Often, by adding ".com" to the company name, you'll tap into its Web site. Morningstar, mentioned earlier, offers a Web site that provides important data you should look at before investing.

You'll often see mutual funds advertising that they have a five-star rating. This is the top rating that only a small percentage of the funds receive. The rating scale moves from a high of five stars to a low of one star. The Morningstar rating is a reflection of risk-adjusted performance. Remember, however, that past performance is not necessarily indicative of how the fund will perform in the future. According to a Morningstar analyst, the star rating should just be a starting point in weeding out which mutual fund to buy.

The Morningstar rating doesn't tell you if a particular fund is the right one to meet your specific goals. It doesn't give the details of the strategy or investment philosophy of the fund manager. In addition, the rating doesn't tell you how well a fund has done in a particular type of economic environment. Nevertheless, it's an extremely helpful tool to use when you're deciding which mutual fund to buy.

There's also the old-fashioned way to identify mutual funds in which to invest, books and magazines. Gene Walden's book, *The 100 Best Mutual Funds to Own in America* (Dearborn 1998), is an excellent starting point. In addition, financial and business publications always offer tips on which mutual funds are performing well. Recommendations, however, are just the beginning.

The best way to learn about a mutual fund is by reading the prospectus. It contains the most current information about a fund's investment objective, as well as policies it operates by and risks. The prospectus is an extremely useful tool.

By reading the prospectus, you'll get the low-down on sales loads and annual expenses. You'll see if your investment goals are compatible with the approach taken by the fund manager. You'll learn if the fund is suitable for someone with your investment temperament.

You'll find the prospectus isn't an incomprehensible document. It's designed to be easy to read and understand. Mutual funds are participating in the U.S. Securities and Exchange Commission's "plain English" initiative. The SEC has mandated that companies prepare all investment materials in plain English by December 1, 1999. The goal is to provide investors with a prospectus that is easy to read and understand. Of course, the IRS often attempts to write its rules and regulations in plain English, so don't feel too bad if you have to reread the prospectus a few times.

The new and improved prospectuses will use active, not passive voice. They will contain shorter sentences and will avoid legal jargon. There will be lists of bullet points for complex material. The end result is that prospectuses will be shorter and you'll stay awake longer when reading them. In addition, thousands of trees that might have become prospectuses will be spared.

The SEC has also changed its disclosure requirements. The prospectus must include risk information such as volatility analysis. But gone are fascinating topics like shareholder voting requirements.

Along with the prospectus, mutual funds are permitted to use a simplified *fund profile*. The profile is generally a three- to six-page document that will provide a wealth of information about the fund. You can learn more about the these issues on the SEC Web site (www.sec.gov). The SEC's toll-free line is 800-SEC-0330 (800-732-0330).

TIPS ON INVESTING FOR RETIREMENT

As we mentioned earlier, an important element in any early retirement strategy is how you invest your money. Obviously, it's not enough to cut your budget and save your pennies. It's just as important to find the right investment vehicle for your money and start her up.

It's unlikely you'll be able to retire early by signing up for savings bond payroll deduction at work. Similarly, it's not enough to just sign up for your employer's 401(k) retirement savings plan. You still must choose the right mix of investments within that 401(k) retirement savings plan. Although there are cases of employees getting rich by investing all of their savings in the employer's stock, it's usually not the wisest move. You're putting all of your eggs in one basket and you already depend on your employer for eggs every payday.

As a general rule, a mutual fund is better than an investment in a single stock because it spreads the risk. Although you won't necessarily make the big score that comes with an individual stock that goes through the roof, your chances of outpacing inflation are good. With a mutual fund, your money is pooled with investments from other shareholders. It is professionally managed by experts whose full-time job is selecting the best investments that meet the mutual fund's objectives.

Whether you're investing in mutual funds or individual stocks, it pays to reinvest your earnings. With a mutual fund, you may receive dividends and capital gains with which you can buy more shares. By reinvesting the dividends from individual stocks, you can also buy more shares that will generate more dividends. Due to compounding, your rate of growth will accelerate.

In Chapter 2, I looked at the psychology of money. Many people aren't risk takers and can't deal with taking chances with their money. They'll stare at the ceiling nightly, wondering if they've done the right thing. Nevertheless, you can take on more risk and still have peace of mind.

With mutual fund investing, the dollar cost averaging strategy can reduce your risk. It's a systematic investment program whereby you invest the same amount at regular intervals. By investing the same amount each month, you'll buy more shares when prices are low and less shares when prices are high. Over the long haul, as long as you don't deviate from the schedule, you're likely to end up with a favorable price per share. By doing so, you'll reduce your risk.

You'll also reduce your risk by minimizing the fees you pay. Some mutual funds are no load, which means you don't pay a front-end or back-end sales commission. Others sock you with a significant fee that is taken out when the shares are purchased or when you sell. The load is essentially a commission for the person who sold you the fund.

Some funds charge a 12b-1 fee. Technically, it's a fee for advertising, marketing, and distribution costs. A true no-load fund won't have a 12b-1 fee. These fees are an indirect way of compensating the broker and covering commissions paid to salespeople. 12b-1 fees can be significant.

Even if you invest in a no-load fund, examine the operating expenses. Your rate of return may be reduced if the operating expenses are too high. Look for a highly-rated fund that has operating expenses of 1 percent or less. These fees can make an enormous difference in your investment account over the years. According to SEC chairman Arthur Levitt, a fee of 1 percent will reduce an investor's final account balance by 17 percent on an investment held for 20 years.

INVESTING FUNDS THAT AREN'T IN YOUR RETIREMENT ACCOUNT

As I've stressed before, the early retirement strategy for each person will be a little bit different. People who are absolutely certain they won't retire until 59½ can plow more money into retirement savings accounts. Although everyone should take advantage of the maximum IRA contribution of $2,000, as well as retirement savings plans at work, people who will retire earlier than 59½ need additional funds that aren't locked away. These people need a liquid source of capital, so they won't incur penalties by tapping retirement accounts prematurely. Doing so will reduce your retirement savings designated for after age 59½.

Most people won't be able to retire early with their ready cash tied up in conservative mutual funds. They'll need to invest aggressively to build an account to live on prior to age 59½. If you can't cope with more aggressive investments, you'll need to put away more money from your paycheck and cut your budget further.

Along with aggressive investing, you can take advantage of the reduced capital gains rate of 20 percent for assets held more than 12 months. Capital gains taxes are normally due on the sale of an asset, such as stock, that has appreciated in value. Previously, the top rate was 28 percent. The capital gains rate is important, because some people will need to invest aggressively if they want to retire sooner or have waited too long to start saving for retirement.

Under the Taxpayer Relief Act of 1997, the maximum rate of tax on a net capital gain is lower for most sales. A net capital gain is the amount by which your net long-term capital gain for the year is greater than your net short-term capital loss. Naturally, it gets more complicated, so you might need to see an accountant. Remember that losses on stocks must be applied to gains in the same category. Short-term losses must be applied against short-term gains. Long-term losses must be applied against long-term gains.

This break is extremely important, because not all of your money will be sheltered in an individual retirement account (IRA) or retirement savings plan. You'll need lots of ready cash to bridge the gap from the time the paychecks stop until you're 59½ or you can start drawing pension or Social Security checks. Once you're where you want to be, you're better off with a diversified portfolio, so a plunge in the market won't unretire you.

As you get closer to your early retirement date, the money you need for the first two to three years should be in conservative investments like money market funds or government bond funds. The money you won't need for five or six years should be invested more aggressively. The money from aggressive and riskier mutual funds should be gradually moved to more conservative investments. One possibility is taking the capital gains from the riskier funds and moving them to more conservative ones.

Some people consider themselves adept at investing. One early retiree was able to supplement his income through shrewd investing. It's a lot harder, however, when there's no bull market pushing stocks up. If there's a bear market, you're going to have a bear of time retiring.

ASSET ALLOCATION

Asset allocation is a strategy of dividing your investments among different types of assets such as stocks, bonds, and cash. Essentially, it's based upon the premise that by diversifying your investments, you'll do better in the long run. Advocates of asset allocation believe that the most significant factor in determining your investment success isn't which investment you choose, but what percentage you've allocated for stocks, bonds, and cash.

Asset allocation reduces your risk and will be an important part of your strategy to retire early. The idea is to find the right mix of investments to achieve early retirement. Depending on how well you're doing, you'll change your mix of investments periodically. Your money will be spread among asset classes such as stocks, bonds, and money market funds. Although one asset class may decline in value, the broad diversification among asset classes reduces the overall volatility of your portfolio.

In another era, as people neared retirement, financial advisers screamed to switch to more conservative investments. Even if you aren't going to retire early, a lot of the screaming is going the other way today. Older people are cautioned against being too conservative with their investments. If you have 30 years of retirement ahead of you, it stands to reason that you'll need more aggressive investments.

The old maxim used to be that there's a mathematical equation to determine how much of your money should be in the stock market. Subtract your age from 100. The result is the percentage of your funds that should be in the market. If you're 70, 30 percent of your money should be in the market. If you're 30, 70 percent of your funds should be in equity investments.

Most financial planners have abandoned this rule of thumb. 70 year olds may have a long life ahead of them. If inflation kicks in, they will find their purchasing power reduced. Even older people may need to invest aggressively to ensure that they live comfortably in retirement.

Asset allocation makes certain your portfolio is right for your personal situation, such as your age and your goals. By having the right mix of investments, you reduce your risk and increase the possibility of producing a favorable rate of return. With mutual funds, you can diversify your portfolio so you're not totally dependent on investments that are losing value. A good financial planner can help you balance your portfolio. If you want to make a go of it on your own, many personal finance magazines offer sample portfolios for individuals in various age brackets with similar financial objectives. Remember, too, that each year you must rebalance your portfolio if jumps or declines in value cause it to become out of sync.

As part of their 401(k) investment options, some companies handle the asset allocation for you. For example, one fund offered by Bank of America is called the Target 2015 Fund. The Fund

> seeks to provide the highest return possible consistent with the average risk tolerance of investors expecting to utilize funds in the year 2015. The Fund utilizes a broad array of securities representing a wide range of asset classes. The allocation among the particular asset classes is managed in a dynamic fashion— reducing overall portfolio risk as the year 2015 approaches.

For those who hope to utilize their retirement account in 2025, a different portfolio is structured. Once again, as the target year approaches, the Fund manager invests in assets that are less risky. Along with the Target 2015 Fund and Target 2025 Fund, the Target 2035 Fund is for those investors who won't be utilizing their funds until the year 2035.

Charles Schwab, the financial services firm, offers portfolios that make it easier for investors to utilize the asset allocation strategy. These funds offer broad diversification across asset classes. There is a conservative asset allocation portfolio that invests in a target asset mix of 40 percent stocks, 55 percent bonds, and 5 percent cash equivalents.

The balanced portfolio focuses more on equities. There is also a portfolio that offers aggressive asset allocation that has a target mix of 80 percent stocks. The most aggressive portfolio has a target mix of 100 percent stocks that includes U.S. large-cap, U.S. small-cap, and international stocks. By doing so, the fund creates a balance within your stock portfolio, even though true asset allocation utilizes a balance of different assets like stocks, bonds, and cash.

Almost everyone has heard the advice that you need to put away money to cover three to six months of living expenses in an emergency fund. If you're laid off, lose your job, or become disabled, this emergency fund can be a godsend. It can help you get through a very difficult period. Before you begin investing, you need to have a fully-funded emergency fund to cover at least three to six months of living expenses. Otherwise, if you run into a problem, you may be forced to tap your retirement account prematurely or sell investments when they're at a low point.

When you retire at a traditional age, you'll still need an emergency fund that you can access whenever necessary. Normally, there's less danger of an interruption in your income, because you're not dependent on a paycheck. Usually, you'll have Social Security and pension payments coming in each month. Nevertheless, if you're dependent on investments and savings for part of your income, and most of those assets are tied up in stock, you'll need more than three to six months in cash reserve.

Let's say you only have one year in ready cash. If there's a bear market, a year may not be enough time for the value of your investments to recover. Unless you have a large cash reserve, you'll be forced to liquidate stock at the wrong time.

If you retire earlier than the traditional retirement age, you'll need an even larger stash of cash to carry you through the bad times. The reason is that you won't have pension checks and Social Security to help subsidize your lifestyle each month. When the time comes that you're living on your investments instead of working for a paycheck, you'll need a lot more than three to six months of savings.

Personal finance guru Jane Bryant Quinn offered advice on how to allocate your investments when you're a younger retiree. Quinn suggested putting enough cash into short-term money market instruments to cover three years of living expenses. With that cushion in place, you can then allocate the rest of your assets into stocks and other investments with growth potential.

This safety net makes it possible for you to allocate more money into equity investments. Otherwise, you may be forced to liquidate a portion of your investments when the market is in a slump. One certified financial planner recommends that you never put money that you'll need in less than five years into stock.

ANNUITIES

Annuities are touted as a way to ensure that you'll have a guaranteed income for life. An annuity is a contract between you and an insurance company. You make one premium payment or a series of payments and the insurance company pays out money to you on an agreed on schedule, now or at a later date. If you want payments to begin immediately, you would opt for an immediate annuity.

A typical arrangement is the single premium deferred annuity. You make one premium payment of $10,000 or more. The earnings on the payment grow on a tax-deferred basis. When you're ready to retire, you choose the payout option that meets your need for retirement income. If you're 59½, you'll only be taxed on the earnings withdrawn.

The insurance company doesn't do this out of the goodness of its heart. It expects to earn more on your money than it will pay out. In addition, there are mortality and expense charges deducted.

You can choose between a fixed-rate annuity or a variable annuity. The danger with a fixed-rate annuity is that the rate is only guaranteed for one year. If the rate goes down, the surrender charge may force you to hold on to the annuity. The surrender charge is a penalty assessed against the accumulated cash value of the annuity if you want to pull your money out.

A recent advertisement for an annuity featured a 7 percent interest rate in bold print. In smaller type, the ad pointed out that the 7 percent interest rate included a 1.5 percent first year bonus. The bonus, however, is paid at the insurance company's discretion and may be withdrawn after the first year. In even smaller print, the ad mentioned that the subsequent renewal interest rate would be no less than 3 percent.

The annuity advertised was available by stopping in at one of a local bank's branches. In recent years, banks were permitted to offer annuities to customers. Even though you can buy an annuity through your bank, the investment is not FDIC (Federal Deposit Insurance Corporation) or FSLIC (Federal

Savings and Loan Insurance Corporation) insured. The financial institution is not in any way guaranteeing the performance of the insurer that actually issues the annuity.

The guaranty association in your state does offer some protection for your annuity, but it's not the same as being insured by the FDIC or FSLIC. It can be quite difficult to collect from a guaranty association. You may not be able to withdraw funds as quickly as you desire, and the interest rate may be reduced.

Many annuity investors aren't content with a fixed rate of return. They are willing to purchase a variable annuity, which offers many investment options. With a variable annuity, you, not the insurance company, control how your funds are invested. If you want to switch investments, you can do so easily without any tax ramifications. Along with these investment options come varying degrees of risk. Normally, the annuity company will offer dozens of mutual funds. If you're willing to take the risk and invest aggressively, the variable annuity can produce a much higher rate of return than a fixed-rate annuity.

The problem with variable annuities is the fees. Along with the fees for insurance, you're paying mutual fund management fees. According to Morningstar, which tracks annuities and mutual funds, a variable annuity has insurance expenses that average 1.27 percent per year. The average mutual fund expense is 0.82 percent per year. Therefore, the combined average variable annuity fees and expenses are over 2 percent.

Think long and hard before buying an annuity. There is also a surrender charge if you want to cash out of the annuity early. The surrender charge is the insurance company's way of recapturing the commission it paid to the salesperson. The penalty is clearly stated in the annuity contract. Usually, the surrender charge will go down each year. The surrender charge won't totally vanish until about the seventh year of the contract.

The annuity contract should allow for partial withdrawals, however. Typically, you can take out 10 percent of the accumulated cash value in a year. This provision in the contract will be useful if you need to tap the annuity for funds during the years the surrender charge is in effect. In addition to the penalties imposed by the contract, taking money from an annuity may result in tax penalties as well.

Under section 1035 of the Internal Revenue Code, you can exchange one annuity for another tax free. For example, you may want to exchange a fixed-rate annuity for a variable annuity, if you're unhappy with the rate of return. Another possibility is that you're concerned about the financial health of the insurance company from which you purchased the annuity. Though you won't pay taxes on the exchange, you still have the surrender charge issue.

Under the new law, capital gains are taxed at a reduced rate. With a variable annuity, you hope your investments result in large amounts of capital gains. Unfortunately, when you withdraw money, it's taxed as regular income. You don't get the capital gains tax break, which is one criticism of annuities.

Annuities are a retirement investment that won't resolve the problem of your need for cash prior to age 59½. There are penalties if you withdraw money prior to that age in most instances. Buying an annuity may increase your post–59½ income, but will reduce the amount you have on hand to retire earlier. The money you put in an annuity will limit the funds you have to make the transition from your early retirement date until age 59½. In addition, you really shouldn't consider an annuity until you've exhausted the other retirement savings options such as IRAs and 401(k)s.

EVALUATING THE COMPANY OFFERING THE ANNUITY

If you're shopping for an annuity, it's important to find a company you trust. You may not be tapping the annuity for many years, so you'll want a company that is financially stable and likely to be around when you need it. Fortunately, you don't have to examine the company's books yourself. There are independent rating services that scrutinize the financial well-being of insurance companies.

One of the most prominent independent rating organizations is A.M. Best. It provides an independent opinion of an insurance company's ability to meet its obligation to policyholders. Although a few highly-rated companies have run into financial problems, the A.M. Best rating can be extremely helpful in evaluating the financial strength of an insurance company.

A.M. Best assigns two types of rating opinions, a letter grade ranging from A++ to F or a Financial Performance Rating (FPR) ranging from a high of 9 to a low of 1. The letter grade represents an opinion that is based on a comprehensive quantitative and qualitative evaluation of an insurance company's financial strength, operating performance, and market profile. The FPR is A.M. Best's opinion, based on a quantitative evaluation of a company's financial strength and operating performance. As a general rule, FPRs are assigned to small or new companies.

Under the A.M. Best rating system, A++ means the carrier has a superior rating. A+ is also a superior rating. A and A– are considered to be excellent ratings. B++ and B+ are very good ratings. A++ through B+ are viewed as Secure Best's Ratings. Grades below B+ are classified as Vulnerable Best's Ratings.

In lieu of a letter grade rating, a company will receive an FPR rating. An FPR 9 rating is indicative of a very strong company. FPR 8 and FPR 7 are strong ratings. FPR 6 and FPR 5 are good ratings. A.M. Best classifies these FPR 9 through FPR 5 ratings as secure. Ratings below 5 are considered vulnerable. FPR 4 is viewed as fair. FPR 3 is considered marginal. FPR 2 is a weak rating. As you might expect, FPR 1 is a poor rating.

When you're shopping for an annuity, insist on a company with a secure rating from A.M. Best. The higher the rating, the better off you are. If it were my money, I'd choose a company with a traditional letter grade of A+ or better.

It's in your best interest to buy a policy from a company that's been in business for a long time. If a company is too new or small to have a rating from A.M. Best, it's a much riskier bet for the purchaser of an annuity.

To find a company's rating, you can visit the A.M. Best Web site at www.ambest.com. The rating can be sent to you by fax or e-mail. The charge is $4.95 for each Best's Rating. You can also contact A.M. Best at 800-424-BEST (800-424-2378) to obtain ratings for a fee. Before paying for this service, however, check with your local library to see if the ratings are available. A good business library will have the latest book of A.M. Best ratings.

There are several other companies that rate the financial stability of insurance carriers. Standard & Poor's Insurance Rating Services range goes from AAA to CC. As of May 11, 1998, Standard & Poor's changed the method by which it rates insurance companies. The claims-paying ability was replaced with financial strength ratings.

Standard & Poor's top rating, AAA, means the company is extremely strong. AA means the company is very strong, and an A reflects that the carrier is strong. Companies with a BBB rating are considered to be in good financial shape. Ratings from Standard & Poor's below BBB means the company is vulnerable.

Standard & Poor's ratings are available through the Insurance News Network, which is on the Internet at www.insure. com. You can also find them in your local library. The Standard & Poor's ratings Web site is www.ratings.com. Standard & Poor's phone number is 212-208-1527.

Duff & Phelps Credit Rating Company in Chicago also offers reports on insurance companies. Though it still utilizes claims-paying ability, the rating is a good indicator of an insurer's financial strength. The rating you should look for is AA or better. The phone number for Duff & Phelps is 312-368-3157. Its Web site is at www.dcrco.com.

Another place to look is Moody's Investor Service, Inc. When looking at the Moody's rating, you should expect to see an AA or better rating. The phone number for Moody's is 212-553-0377. Its Web site is at www.moodys.com.

Weiss Research, Inc., can also be used to research the financial health of an insurer. Weiss Research, as a general rule, provides the most skeptical report on the insurance company's financial well-being. The rating service can be reached at 800-289-9222 or on the Internet at www.weissinc.com.

Your state's insurance department can provide the financial ratings of insurance companies. Due to limited resources, however, that department may not have the latest ratings or be able to supply them at all.

Don't rely on a salesperson to tell you the ratings of the companies from which you're buying a policy. And be wary of an agent who explains away the financial rating of the company backing the annuity by saying that you're protected by the state guaranty fund. Don't ask for problems from the get-go.

PAYOUT OPTIONS WITH ANNUITIES

There are numerous payout options with annuities. You select the one that best meets your needs. The most traditional payout option is the straight life annuity. Based on its assumptions about interest rates and expenses, the insurance company looks at the age of the person who will be paid and the individual's life expectancy. The payout is based on those factors. The person choosing this payout option will receive an income he or she can't outlive.

Is this payout option a good deal? As Dirty Harry would say, "Do you feel lucky? Well, do you punk?" If you die prematurely, the straight life annuity payout option was the wrong choice. But if you outlive the life-span prediction in the actuarial tables, you'll be pleased you chose that particular option.

A way to reduce the risk of this option is choosing the life annuity with term certain. You guarantee that the insurance company will make payments for a specified term. You might choose a 10- or 20-year term certain guarantee. As you might expect, the monthly income will be less than with the straight life annuity. The beneficiary of the annuity contract would receive the remaining income, if you die.

A different way to reduce risk is by selecting a cash refund annuity. This annuity still pays income for life, even if you live to be the world's oldest human being. If you die before all of your premium is paid out, however, the insurer refunds the remainder to your beneficiary in one lump sum. Obviously, your beneficiary would still be on the short end of the deal, because the earnings on the premium are likely to be significant and are lost.

With the installment refund payout option, the result is similar. The difference is that your beneficiary receives income until the principal is paid out. By doing so, the annuity isn't totally wasted. Because the money isn't paid out in one lump sum, your beneficiary can't blow it all at once on something foolish. He or she can blow it gradually on many foolish things.

Another common payout option is the joint-and-survivor annuity. The purpose of this annuity is to pay income for two lives. Even if one of you dies, the annuity payments continue. Because the insurance company is likely to be making payments for a longer period, the monthly payout is less than if that same man or woman chose the straight life annuity. This particular annuity option works well for a husband and wife who are looking for income in retirement.

The payout options can be structured to meet the needs of almost anyone in any situation. Remember, however, that these payouts may seem paltry by the time you get to use them. $600 per month or a similar payout isn't going to let you live like a king in retirement.

As a general rule, once you start taking a life annuity, you can't change your mind about the payout. Some annuity companies are trying to put more flexibility into the payout stage. Ask before signing on the dotted line.

Once you begin receiving payments from your annuity, you'll pay taxes on a portion of them. Part of your payment will be principal, which is not taxable, and the rest will be subject to income tax. Under the Taxpayer Relief Act of 1997, there is a new recovery method used to calculate the tax-free portion of an annuity payable over the lives of more than one individual. The recovery factor is determined by combining the ages of the annuitants. Take a look at IRS Publication 553, but the odds are good you'll need an accountant to help you with this one. The company paying out on the annuity will tell you what portion of your payment is taxable. The IRS Web site is www.irs.ustreas.gov.

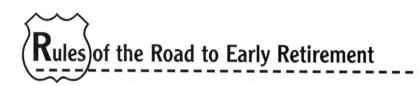

Rules of the Road to Early Retirement

▶ The rule of 72 lets you calculate how long it takes your money to double. You divide 72 by the rate of return you're getting. The result is the number of years it will take to double your money.

▶ Take advantage of the lower capital gains rates. All of the money you're investing for your early retirement won't be sheltered in a retirement account. You'll need lots of cash to take you to the point when you can begin withdrawing funds from your retirement account. One way to get cash is to invest aggressively.

▶ Fees can make an extremely big difference in how well your investments perform. Watch out for loads on mutual funds, which pay for sales commissions. With no-load funds, you pay no front-end or back-end sales charge.

▶ Asset allocation is a strategy for diversifying your investments and couching your bets. By diversifying, you stand a better chance of making money in the long term and reduce your risk of losing ground.

▶ You shouldn't begin investing aggressively until you've established an emergency cash reserve to cover your expenses for at least three to six months. Early retirees need a cash cushion of much longer because they don't have regular sources of income like a pension or Social Security. If early retirees need to sell stocks or mutual fund shares to live on, they risk liquidating those assets at the wrong time.

▶ Don't even think about an annuity until you've exhausted your other retirement options such as 401(k)s and IRAs. If you still have money to put

away for retirement, consider an annuity. If you're shooting for early retirement, however, you'll still have to wait until age 59½ to tap your annuity. While an annuity will increase your income stream after that age,
you'll have less money on hand for the time frame prior to age 59½. A
big advantage with annuities is that there's no cap on the amount you can
invest, unlike 401(k)s and IRAs.

▶ If you opt for a fixed-rate annuity, be wary of bonuses that are only guaranteed for the first year. Bonuses are paid at the insurance company's discretion and may be discontinued. The subsequent guaranteed renewal
rate may be percentage points lower. With a variable annuity, you're actually buying an insurance policy that is tied to an investment portfolio.

▶ Remember that annuities are not insured by the FDIC, even if you buy
them at a bank. Always check one or more insurer rating services before
buying an annuity. The company backing the annuity should be in tip-top
financial shape. Don't rely on the fact that there is a guaranty fund in your
state.

≈ Retirement Savings Plans

After my parents moved to Florida in the mid-1980s, Mom and Dad would send us the job ads from the Sunday newspaper. In one letter, Mom circled an ad that she thought was perfect. "Look at this one," she wrote. "It pays $401,000." On closer inspection, we realized the job offered a 401(k) retirement savings plan, not a $401,000 salary.

Unfortunately, no one in our family ever came close to making $401,000 per year. If you're in the same boat, you can still retire early. The trick is taking full advantage of a 401(k) or any other retirement savings plan available to you.

A recent survey found that nearly half of people polled believe they won't be able to afford to retire. The survey, which was commissioned by SunAmerica, Inc., and the Teresa & H. John Heinz III Foundation, found that people age 25 to 55 believe they won't have enough money saved for retirement. The individuals surveyed feel this way because they are unable to save money now. Perhaps, as a public service, someone should have told the participants in the survey about 401(k) retirement savings plans.

Of course, I'm amazed they could find anyone willing to participate in a survey. Every call I get that purports to be a survey ends with a sales pitch for aluminum siding. If someone called me to participate in a survey regarding retirement, I would assume a broker or insurance salesperson is on the other end of the line.

Whether you're shooting for early retirement or retirement at a more typical age, 401(k) retirement saving plans will be a key element of your strategy. About 25 million Americans are now participating in 401(k) plans. If you're not among them, you should be.

In 1992, 18.5 million workers participated in 401(k)s and had $410 billion invested. According to the Spectrem Group in San Francisco, Americans have now stashed away over $1 trillion in 401(k) retirement savings plans as of March, 1998. Though much of that increase in assets might be attributed to the booming stock market, more workers are taking advantage of this tax break.

That trillion dollars doesn't include the $420 billion invested in 403(b) and 457 plans. Section 457 plans are for employees of state and local government, as well as certain individuals who work for tax-exempt organizations. Section 403(b) plans are tax-sheltered annuity programs for employees of public schools, colleges, and certain not-for-profit organizations. These plans are very similar to 401(k)s.

With all of these plans, employees defer a percentage of their salary and invest the money in tax-sheltered retirement accounts. The money is put aside before taxes are taken out. The funds inside the accounts grow and aren't taxed until withdrawn.

Along with the tax break, most employers throw in a contribution of their own. Depending on the company, the employer may kick in a specified amount for each dollar the employee puts in the 401(k). A typical match is 50 cents for each dollar the employee contributes. Naturally, the employer will only provide this match up to a specified percentage of the employee's pay, usually 6 percent.

401(k) retirement savings plans with matching contributions from the employer help companies retain employees. The employer's contribution may not vest for a specified number of years, which gives employees an incentive to stay. With most plans, you're not eligible for the 401(k) until you've been employed at the company for one year.

With 401(k)s, there is a maximum amount that you can put away each year. Whether you're Bill Gates or making minimum wage, the rules pertaining to participants in the company 401(k) are the same for every member of the plan. Your net worth won't approach his, but your 401(k)s will be playing by the same rules.

To retire early, one of the best approaches is to make the maximum tax-deferred contribution allowable. The maximum is currently $10,000 or a lower ceiling established by the plan. Although your employer may only match a portion of that contribution, you'll still build an enormous tax-sheltered account. Because you're funding the account with pre-tax dollars, you'll pay fewer taxes now. The 401(k) and similar plans are the best ways to fund the post–59½ stage of your retirement. The employer's contribution makes a big difference as you can see in the chart below.

Worker Earning $30,000 Annually
Contributing 5% of Pay ($1,500)
Annual Rate of Return 4%
Employer Match of 50%

Age	Before match	After match	Difference	% of difference
25	$ 1,560	$ 2,340	$ 780	50%
30	10,347	15,521	5,174	50
35	21,039	31,558	10,519	50
40	34,046	51,069	17,023	50
45	49,872	74,808	24,936	50
50	69,126	103,689	34,563	50
55	92,552	138,828	46,276	50
60	121,053	181,580	60,527	50
65	155,729	233,594	77,865	50

SOURCE: American Savings Education Council

You'll only be entitled to the employer's contribution if you're vested. Always check with your plan administrator to find out when you'll be vested. At that point, the employer's contribution becomes yours forever.

YOU CAN TAKE IT WITH YOU

Unlike past eras, it's doubtful you'll spend your career with the same employer. When you're ready to move on, you'll face some important decisions about what to do with your 401(k) plan. Essentially, there are four choices when you're ready to take a hike:

1. Take the money and run.
2. Leave the money in your employer's plan.
3. Move the money to your new employer's plan.
4. Roll the money over into an IRA.

Taking the money is usually the worst choice. You may be hit with a 10 percent penalty, as well as federal and possibly state taxes on the money. You'll also lose thousands of dollars down the road because that money won't be growing in the tax-sheltered account. Even a small amount of money will grow significantly over the years. Research shows that people with small distributions usually do not roll them over into a retirement account.

A second option is to leave the money where it is. This makes sense if your former employer offers investment choices that appeal to you. Make sure there are no administrative fees for non-employees and that the rules are basically the same. If your 401(k) account is small, you may be forced to take the money elsewhere. If you leave the money where it is, there are no tax consequences.

If you're going to work elsewhere, consider transferring your lump-sum distribution to the new employer's plan. Most companies with 401(k) plans will accept rollovers from your previous employer. Because you're rolling the money from one plan to another, you won't pay any taxes.

If you're finished working or you don't like the investment choices at your new employer, the money can be transferred directly to an IRA at a bank, brokerage firm, or mutual fund company. It's best for the money to be transferred directly from your employer to the new IRA. Otherwise, the employer will be required to withhold 20 percent and you might also get smacked with the 10 percent early withdrawal penalty.

The safest bet is a direct rollover to an IRA. The IRS is happy, because you haven't touched the money. If you take possession of the funds, the money must be rolled over within 60 days or you face some significant tax consequences. As a general rule, if you're under age 59½, you'll pay a stiff 10 percent penalty in addition to the normal taxes on the money withdrawn.

It's important to note that you can't roll over your money directly into a Roth IRA, which allows tax free withdrawals. If money were to go directly to the Roth IRA, the IRS wouldn't get its hands on any of it. Because your 401(k) contributions were made before taxes were taken out, the government won't let that money find its way to a tax-free account until its share is taken.

TAX TREATMENT OF DISTRIBUTIONS

Many distributions from retirement savings plans never find their way into IRAs. Many distributions, especially small ones, wind up in the departing employee's wallet or purse. The recipients forget that this is money for their retirement, not an unexpected windfall they're getting as a going away present from their former employer.

Aside from the 10 percent penalty, taking a lump-sum distribution from a retirement savings plan can have serious tax ramifications. Unless you roll the distribution over into an IRA, you'll pay a significant tax bill. If you're age 59½, you can use five-year averaging to soften the blow. It is described in IRS Form 4972. Five-year averaging is scheduled to be eliminated in the year 2000, which might not matter because the IRS computers probably won't be working anyway.

There are some different rules for distributions from plans that include the employer's stock. You may have the option of avoiding tax on the net unrealized appreciation of the stock until after you sell it. If this option is facing you, it may be time to call Cousin Sid, the CPA.

IGNORANCE IS BLISS

Financial experts are concerned that many employees have no idea how to invest the money in their 401(k) retirement account. Employees are selecting investments they don't understand. Companies, however, are fearful of giving investment advice that could lead to a lawsuit. If advice is offered, it is usually quite general.

Blue Shield of California recently began offering online investment advice to employees who participate in the company's 401(k) plan. The advice is personalized and is quite inexpensive when compared to the cost of a financial planner. The online service helps answer the questions of how much to save and how to invest contributions to the 401(k). Investment recommendations are based on an online questionnaire that determines the individual's risk tolerance, knowledge of investing, and needs.

In many cases, employees are left on their own to invest thousands of dollars each year. The result is that many invest with no consideration of their goals or tolerance for risk. These employees often don't have any kind of strategy.

Many fail to diversify their 401(k) portfolio. Instead, their investment mix isn't much of a mix at all. Frequently, they invest too much money in their employer's stock. As a result, their career and their retirement plan is dependent on the fortunes of one company.

In some cases, sticking with the company stock pays off. On the way to the ocean, my wife and I pass the expensive retirement home of a UPS employee who made millions in the company stock plan. Although he made a relatively low salary during his career, he plowed his money into the company stock and was rewarded handsomely for doing so.

Other 401(k) investors play it much too conservatively and their retirement accounts will barely keep up with inflation. They stick with the fixed-income fund in their 401(k) plan and shun more aggressive investments. If your 401(k) constitutes most of your retirement savings, you need to have a portion of your money invested in stock funds. It's the only way you'll keep pace with inflation.

There is no iron-clad strategy for investing your 401(k) funds. We have discussed asset allocation and your 401(k) should certainly make use of that strategy. If you want to retire soon and you haven't put much money away, you'll have to invest more aggressively. The danger, however, is that you'll lose ground rather than make headway toward the dream of early retirement.

Often, how you invest the funds in your 401(k) is more important than your salary. In one family, the wife made more than her husband throughout her career. Her 401(k) was invested in fixed-income investments, while he invested in stock. Despite the differences in salary, his 401(k) wound up being much larger than hers.

If you're years away from retirement, you should put at least a portion of your 401(k) in stock mutual funds to keep pace with inflation. You'll take advantage of dollar cost averaging, which reduces your risk. With this strategy, you buy more shares when prices are down and less when they're up. In the long run, you'll wind up with a favorable price per share. Nevertheless, if you can't stand to see your 401(k) statement fluctuate from month to month, stick with more conservative investments.

IT'S A RETIREMENT ACCOUNT, NOT AN ATM

It's not just choosing the right investment that helps 401(k)s grow faster. It's keeping your hands off them too. Most plans permit you to borrow against the account balance for compelling reasons. Those all-too-compelling reasons may reduce the amount you'll be able to draw someday from your 401(k).

If retirement, early or otherwise, is your dream, you can't view your 401(k) as a source of ready cash. Many 401(k) plans let you borrow from your assets. Recent statistics indicate that roughly one-third of the participants have loans outstanding. You're charged interest on the loan, but you're paying back the interest to yourself.

Some financial experts encourage borrowing from 401(k)s. They're convinced that 401(k)s are the perfect source of funds to pay for major expenditures that crop up over your lifetime. For example, many people borrow from their 401(k) to pay for a child's education. Money in a 401(k) account is not included in the figures that financial aid officers use to determine an aid package for a student.

Despite the advantages of borrowing from a 401(k), it can be detrimental to your retirement planning. If you leave your job, you're obligated to repay any loans against your retirement account. Many plans require repayment of the loan within 30 days. Failing to pay back a loan might be viewed as a distribution from the account and subject to a 10 percent penalty.

When people borrow from a 401(k) account, they may stop making contributions. In fact, your employer's plan may not permit you to make contributions while a loan is outstanding. To borrow from your employer's plan, you'll need to pay back the money with interest and stick to the payment schedule. Some people may not be able to adhere to that schedule and still contribute to their 401(k). If you can't, you'll lose a lot of money over the years in your 401(k). Furthermore, even though you're paying interest on the loan to yourself, the rate of return may be far less than what you would make in the stock market.

Sometimes, your 401(k) will suffer from a marital dispute. A friend who dreamed of early retirement went through a painful divorce while in his early fifties. He lost half his 401(k) in the divorce.

Changing jobs is another problem that can affect the amount you'll wind up with in your 401(k). According to U.S. Bureau of Labor statistics, working women who are over 25 change jobs every 4.8 years. These job changes inhibit the growth of retirement plans.

You may not be eligible to participate right away at your new place of employment. At many firms, you're not able to participate in the 401(k) plan for at least a year. Losing that opportunity will hurt your retirement savings enormously, especially if you change jobs frequently during your career. On a positive note, more companies have reduced or eliminated the waiting period to enroll in the firm's 401(k) plan. In its ads to attract employees, one national mortgage lender promised 401(k) eligibility after only 30 days.

Though you are always vested for the funds you've invested in the plan, you may not be for your employer's contributions. You might have to wait five years until there's full vesting of your employer's contributions to the plan. Before taking a different job, you should be considering how much you'll lose in your 401(k). One young actuary worked for an insurance company that offered a generous match of her contribution. The woman was shocked at how much money was forfeited from her account when she left before her vesting date.

Employers don't always interpret the plan rules correctly. At a company my wife worked for, the employer withdrew its contribution after she left the company. It refused to respond to her request for information as to why the money was withdrawn from her account with Fidelity Investments. Fidelity washed its hands of the matter and said it was the employer's decision to make. Fortunately, after the Department of Labor intervened, the employer *remembered* that my wife should be credited for service with the parent company and the money was returned to her account.

FORCED SAVINGS

Most people would never build a whale of a 401(k) without being encouraged to save. And it's not your mom or dad ordering you to put money away this time. Your employer encourages you to join its retirement savings programs and even sweetens the pot by making contributions on your behalf. Once you sign the necessary paperwork, your contributions are invested automatically each payday. The money is put away before you get your hands on it.

Even the president is getting in on the act. Speaking at the National Summit on Retirement Savings, President Clinton told employers they can now automatically enroll employees in their 401(k) plans. If employees don't want to join the 401(k) plan, they will be required to opt out. The Treasury Department approved the automatic enrollment. The president expects this approach to increase the percentage of enrollment in 401(k)s to 90 percent. The commander-in-chief believes that his action will force people to save for retirement. And it's quite obvious that many people need a push.

The SunAmerica survey helps illustrate why some people need forced savings programs. Sixty-one percent of women and 53 percent of men reported they usually have little or no money left to save for retirement after paying their bills. With 401(k)s, you don't wait to see what's left over before investing.

The beauty of forced savings is that you're paying yourself first. Many people take a reverse approach to savings. They save what's left of their paycheck, if any. When you depend on your personal initiative to save, it often doesn't happen. You avoid this problem with forced savings. It takes no effort, willpower, or discipline.

401(k)s are the best forced savings vehicle you'll ever find. In time, you won't even know that you're missing money from your paycheck. In fact, your take-home pay won't be much lower, because your salary is reduced by the amount invested in the 401(k) so you'll pay less taxes. You'll get used to living on the lower amount and will be saving painlessly. Over the years, you can accumulate tens of thousands of dollars.

Whether you earn a small paycheck or a large one, 401(k)s are an incredible investment vehicle. If you pull down a big salary, you can put away up to $10,000 year. The ceiling is growing.

The only way to derail a rapidly growing 401(k) is by dropping out of the plan or borrowing money from it. Of course, you must first agree to participate. Don't make the excuse that you don't intend to stay long with your current employer. If you wind up staying there for any length of time, you'll be glad you're in the 401(k).

There are other forced savings vehicles, but 401(k)s and similar plans are the best. If you've tapped them to the max, you might consider others like payroll deduction or automatic investments that are deducted from your checking account. Mutual funds will arrange to take a preauthorized amount from an account to purchase shares.

Another difficult decision is whether to enroll in a 401(k) plan or put the money in an IRA. There are no absolute answers as to which is better. Because your employer is usually kicking in a contribution to the 401(k), that account will grow faster. But ideally, you'll be able to make the maximum contribution to a 401(k) plan, while still contributing to an IRA.

There's still time to build a nest egg, even if you're getting a late start on saving for retirement. Let's look at Rex who's pulling down $65,000 as an engineer. Rex is 40, but looks 39 thanks to Rogaine. His goal is to wind up with $200,000 in his 401(k). Until now, he's found excuses for not enrolling.

Goal—$200,000

Time	Annual Deposit	Total Deposit	Total Earnings	Total Saved
10 Years	$12,077	$120,770	$ 79,230	$200,000
15 Years	6,249	93,735	106,265	200,000
20 Years	3,587	71,740	128,260	200,000

(Based on 9 percent annual return; deposit includes employer contribution.)

SOURCE: T. Rowe Price

OTHER RETIREMENT PLANS

There's a retirement account designed for self-employed individuals or employers who don't have other qualified retirement plans. The Simplified Employee Pension, or SEP plan, can increase the money you have available for retirement. SEP plans are a cross between an IRA and a pension plan. Unlike 401(k) retirement accounts, employee contributions are not permitted. The employer, however, makes a tax-deductible contribution each year for eligible employees.

The employer is not locked in to making a set contribution each year. If profits are down, the employer can forgo making a contribution. But once you decide to make a contribution that year, it must be made on behalf of every eligible employee and each must receive the same percentage. Participants are 100 percent vested at all times.

The maximum allowable percentage is 15 percent of employee compensation or $24,000, whichever is less. The employer has flexibility, however. It can lower the contribution in a given year, as long as every eligible employee receives the same percentage.

SEP plans are particularly good options for self-employed individuals running a side business. Essentially, you make an "employer" contribution to your own SEP plan. It doesn't matter if you have a full-time job and are covered by your employer's retirement plan. Once the account is established, there's very little paperwork. All you need to do is make income from your business, whether it's consulting, freelancing, or some other endeavor.

The Keogh plan has been around a lot longer than the SEP. Keogh's are established by a sole proprietor or partnership. You must make the same contribution to the accounts of eligible participants. Your contribution is usually deductible as a business expense. If your business consists of just you, you'd make the contribution on your own behalf.

Some employers offer SIMPLE-IRA plans. The acronym stands for Savings Incentive Match Plan for Employees. The plan makes it possible for employees to defer and save a portion of their salaries. The employer makes matching contributions. The employer's contribution vests immediately. The SIMPLE-IRA is similar to the 401(k) plan, but is designed for companies with 100 or fewer employees.

It probably doesn't hurt to mention Employee Stock Ownership Plans (ESOPs). This type of plan makes it possible for you to obtain shares of your company's stock. Usually, you'll be able to buy the stock at a much lower price than you'd pay on the open market. That's still no guarantee, however, that you'll make money someday on your investment.

WITHDRAWING MONEY FROM YOUR 401(K)

401(k) plans are an excellent way to build wealth, especially if you opt for equity investments and keep making contributions throughout the years. Someday, you might find yourself having hundreds of thousands of dollars. Unfortunately, you may be wealthy on paper without much paper money in your wallet.

The 59½ rule mentioned earlier rears its ugly head when you hope to withdraw funds from a 401(k). Until you reach that milestone, you'll normally pay a penalty to withdraw money from your 401(k) retirement savings plan. The usual penalty is 10 percent of the amount withdrawn. You'll also pay the standard income tax on the amount you've taken out from the 401(k) plan.

If 59½ is too long to wait to retire, there is a loophole that you can use. No, you don't have to die or become disabled, though both may seem attractive after a particularly bad day at work. You can withdraw money without a penalty at age 55, but only if you retire.

The loophole is a 72(t) withdrawal, which is the section of the Internal Revenue Code on which it is based. The original purpose of this law was to help people in their mid- to late-fifties who were laid off and had difficulty landing another job.

They were able to take their 401(k) money without paying a penalty.

This provision of the tax code is restricted to individuals who are at least 55 when they are separated from service. You must either be terminated or quit at that age or older. Unfortunately, you can't quit before age 55 and then utilize this loophole when you reach 55.

You can take all or part of your 401(k) at that age without penalty. Nevertheless, you will pay income taxes on the proceeds. Instead of taking it all at once, it might be smart to only withdraw whatever is needed to tide you over until age 59½. At age 59½, you can begin your 401(k) withdrawals without penalty and take out exactly what you need each year.

Ironically, 403(b) plans permit periodic withdrawals at any age, as long as you withdraw an amount that is based on your life expectancy. Essentially, you are *annuitizing* your retirement plan, so your savings will last a lifetime. Even though the calculations are based on your life expectancy, they must only continue for at least five years. The 403(b) plan withdrawal rules are similar to those that are applicable to IRAs.

If you're not age 59½, or separated from service at age 55 or older, and your money is in a 401(k), you can roll over your funds into an IRA. Internal Revenue Code section 72(t) permits similar withdrawals from IRAs, without penalty, as long as they're "substantially equal periodic payments," which are based on your life expectancy or the joint life expectancy of you and your spouse. Before even attempting this type of withdrawal, consult with a tax expert, as well as a financial planner, to determine the impact on your long-term retirement savings. We discuss this further in Chapter 7.

Remember that you can't roll over a 401(k) into a Roth IRA, which we will talk about in Chapter 7. The reason is that withdrawals from Roth IRAs are tax-free. In addition, your money must be kept in a Roth IRA for at least five years. If your money is rolled over into a non-Roth IRA, you can make withdrawals that are substantially equal periodic payments. And, as mentioned earlier, you must continue making withdrawals for five years, even if you'd rather not.

According to the IRS, there is no set formula for determining what constitutes substantially equal periodic payments. The agency doesn't calculate how much you're permitted to withdraw. The IRS will recognize any reasonable formula for annuitizing your IRA, if it's based on a realistic rate of return. I discuss three methods of withdrawing money from your IRA in Chapter 7.

Unfortunately, your substantially equal periodic payments may not be enough to live on. On the bright side, you don't want to outlive your money by withdrawing too much. Suppose you have $500,000 in an IRA and a 30-year life expectancy. If you assume a 10 percent rate of return, you may withdraw approximately $4,000 per month. The fewer years you're expected to live, the greater the amount that may be withdrawn.

The danger with this type of withdrawal, however, is that if you live longer than 30 years you will run short of money. In addition, by taking these periodic payments, you may undermine the amount you've put away for your post–59½ stage of retirement. And if your actual rate of return is lower than what you've used to calculate the amount of your withdrawal, you'll run into problems later on. Once you begin taking substantially equal periodic payments, you're required to do so for a minimum of five years. The withdrawals must continue, even if you're in no need of the money.

THE MOTHER OF ALL 401(K)S

As we've seen, there are ways to get at your 401(k) before age 59½. If you're separated from service at age 55 or older, you can take the entire account without a penalty. You will, however, pay a whole lot of income taxes. Nevertheless, if your retirement savings plan is huge, and many are because of the stock market surge, you may have enough money to live on for the rest of your life.

There are even some people who may think they can withdraw funds, pay a penalty, and still live on what's left. This is the worst possible strategy, even if you're able to get by on what's left after paying the taxes and the penalty. The price is too high. This course of action will make an enormous dent in your 401(k) because you'll be withdrawing much more than necessary to make up for the penalty. This tactic will inevitably hurt you down the road because your 401(k) will be much less than it would be otherwise.

You'll be working a lot of years to build a great 401(k). You've worked too hard and put up with too much grief to pay penalties on 401(k) withdrawals. Early retirement will never live up to your expectations if you make that kind of sacrifice to have it. Even if you have the mother of all 401(k)s, this is a road you don't want to go down.

Rules of the Road to Early Retirement

▶ Retirement savings plans are the ideal retirement investment, especially when your employer is making contributions to the account. You make your contributions with pretax dollars, so the impact on your take-home pay is less.

▶ If you're eligible and your employer offers a 401(k) retirement savings plan, sign up before the day is over. If you're in your pajamas and getting ready for bed, make it the first thing you do tomorrow. If you're already enrolled in a 401(k) or similar plan, up your contribution by at least a percentage point unless you're at the maximum amount allowed.

▶ Pay particular attention to the vesting requirements of your plan. It may be five years until you're fully vested for the amount that your employer has contributed. If you're less than 100 percent vested, you'll forfeit your employer's contribution if you go elsewhere to work. Even if you start a job and don't expect to stay long, sign up for the 401(k).

▶ Unless you're close to retirement age, you should be putting a large portion of your contribution in a stock mutual fund. No matter how well your company is doing, it's dangerous to invest exclusively in your employer's stock. Your paycheck and your investments will all be tied to the fortunes of one company.

▶ If you're guaranteed a pension, you can take more risks with your 401(k). Always look at the time horizon for your investments. If you don't need the money for 25 years, you can put most of your money in stock mutual funds and feel confident that you'll do well over the long haul.

▶ The 401(k) and similar plans are the best ways to put aside funds for the post–59½ stage of retirement. They offer opportunities for medium-income wage earners to save huge amounts for their retirement years.

▶ One element of our strategy for retiring early is to work part time or have a small side business that brings in an income. If you are going to turn a hobby into a business, there are advantages to starting the business while you're still employed. You can find out if owning a business is enjoyable or more aggravation than you care to deal with. If you're making money from your side business, you can open a SEP plan. It will give you an additional retirement account to draw from later.

▶ There are ways to access 401(k) retirement savings plans prior to age 59½ without a penalty. Consult with an accountant who's extremely knowledgeable in this area. The rules are quite tricky.

7

~

≈ Individual Retirement Accounts

In an ad for Charles Schwab, the financial services firm, the president of the company is quoted. "The first investment I make every year is the $2,000 I put in my IRA," says Schwab. It would be a safe bet he puts that $2,000 in a Schwab individual retirement account (IRA).

Many people don't make that first investment of the year, or any investment for that matter. They never get around to funding an IRA or putting money away in a retirement savings vehicle. Retirement seems too far off to worry about and more pressing needs come first. And it's not just low-income people who have this attitude. Many people earning a nice buck never get around to investing for their retirement.

The Taxpayer Relief Act of 1997 added more options to planning for retirement. One of them is the Roth IRA, named after Senator Roth who introduced it. If you barely understand the rules governing a traditional IRA, you might not realize how the Roth IRA differs. With a traditional IRA, your contributions are fully or partially deductible. Your earnings are also free from federal income taxes until withdrawn. The Roth IRA offers no tax deduction.

In the magazine ad mentioned above, Schwab poses a few questions to help you determine which IRA is better for you. According to Schwab, if you earn less than $110,000 single or $160,000 married per year, you qualify for a Roth IRA and "probably should consider taking advantage of it." I have a hunch Schwab makes too much to qualify for a Roth IRA and contributes to a nondeductible IRA.

While "probably should consider" isn't the strongest endorsement, the Roth IRA has some significant advantages. With a traditional IRA, taxes are deferred until you withdraw the money. On the other hand, with the Roth IRA, withdrawals are tax-free if you play by the rules.

The rules are relatively simple. Your maximum annual contribution is $2,000 or 100 percent of your compensation. Compensation is earned income that includes alimony. A nonworking spouse may make a $2,000 contribution to a Roth IRA as long as the spouse who does work earns more than their combined contribution. Although contributions aren't deductible, withdrawals are tax-free as long as you're older than 59½ and the account has been open for more than five years.

You can even get at your money sooner in certain instances. If you're disabled, you can tap into your Roth IRA before age 59½. You can also withdraw up to $10,000 if the money is used to buy your first home or the first home of someone in your immediate family.

You don't even need a good reason to take money out of your Roth IRA. The actual amount you've contributed, not the earnings, can be withdrawn at any time without tax or penalty. This provision gives you some flexibility, so all your money isn't tied up until age 59½.

With a Roth IRA, you can even work past 70½ and still contribute, though that's probably not going to be of interest to readers of a book about early retirement. You also aren't required to make withdrawals at any age.

And there's good news for your heirs. They can inherit your Roth IRA without paying any income taxes. Just think. They'll be able to retire early should something bad happen to you before your retirement.

Unlike 401(k) retirement savings plans, you fund your Roth IRA with after-tax dollars. Hopefully, you won't need to choose between investing in a 401(k) plan and a Roth IRA. To retire early, you should fund both. If your employer matches the contribution you make to a 401(k), take full advantage of it. Because your employer is adding money to your contribution, it will grow much faster than a Roth IRA. Once you reach the point when your employer stops matching your contribution, deciding between a 401(k) and a Roth IRA is more difficult.

Ideally, you'll be able to make the maximum contribution to a 401(k) plan, while still contributing to a Roth IRA. But, unlike the Roth IRA, you'll pay taxes when money is withdrawn from a 401(k). And even if your 401(k) is totally invested in stocks, you'll pay the ordinary income tax rate, not the reduced tax rate on capital gains brought about by the Taxpayer Relief Act of 1997.

For many people, investing in a 401(k) takes less will power than any IRA. As mentioned earlier, you sign the paperwork and your employer does the rest. Nevertheless, you can force yourself to fund an IRA. According to James O'Shaughnessy who manages two mutual funds, a simple solution is to have the money automatically withdrawn from your checking account each month and put into your IRA. He points out that a $2,000 per year contribution amounts to only $5.50 each day.

Procrastination doesn't pay when it comes to putting money in your IRA. Compare the results below:

Irene, Age 21	Cousin Ira, Age 31
Saves $2,000 per Year	Saves $2,000 per Year
from Age 21 to 30	from Age 31 to 65
(10 Deposits)	(35 Deposits)
Her IRA at Age 65 = $620,296	His IRA at Age 65 = $431,422
(Based on 9% annual	(Based on 9% annual
return)	return)

By starting early, Irene will have a much larger IRA with far fewer contributions. In either case, both Irene and her cousin will have sizable IRAs at age 65. And if Irene continues saving beyond her thirtieth birthday, she'll be well positioned for retirement, early or otherwise.

CHOOSING BETWEEN THE TRADITIONAL IRA AND THE ROTH IRA

Prior to the passage of the Taxpayer Relief Act of 1997, choosing an IRA wasn't difficult. You simply deposited money in a traditional IRA. If you qualified, you took a full or partial tax deduction. If you didn't qualify for a tax deduction, you were still permitted to make a nondeductible contribution.

Even after the creation of the Roth IRA, the nondeductible IRA still exists. It exists primarily for people who can't deduct contributions to a traditional IRA and make too much money to be eligible for a Roth IRA. According to almost every expert, if you qualify for a Roth IRA, you're better off with that than a nondeductible IRA. Your choice is more difficult, however, if you can get a tax deduction for making a contribution to a traditional IRA (see the chart at the end of Chapter 13).

Your contributions to a traditional IRA are deductible for federal income tax purposes if you or your spouse is not an active participant in an employer-maintained plan. As a general rule, you're considered to be an active participant if you participate in an employer's pension, profit-sharing, 401(k), 403(b), or Keogh plan during any part of the year, even if you're not vested yet. However, if neither you nor your spouse is an active participant in an employer's retirement plan, your contributions to a traditional IRA are fully deductible, regardless of your income level.

If you or your spouse is covered by an employer-maintained retirement plan, you can still make a deductible contribution to a traditional IRA if your adjusted gross income is less than $41,000 single or $61,000 married. And the eligibility for tax-deductible IRA contributions will expand each year. In 2007, if your adjusted gross income is less than $100,000, married couples filing jointly will still get a full or partial deduction. In 2005, single taxpayers will still qualify for a deductible IRA contribution if their adjusted gross income is less than $60,000.

Suppose one spouse is an active participant in an employer-sponsored retirement plan and the other spouse isn't. The new law allows the spouse who doesn't participate to make a fully deductible contribution to an IRA. For example, a nonworking spouse can make a fully deductible contribution to a traditional IRA, as long as the spouse who does work earns enough income to cover that contribution. However, the couple's adjusted gross income must be less than $150,000.

Under prior law, the nonparticipating spouse was viewed as an active participant and couldn't make a full or partially deductible contribution, unless the couple's adjusted gross income was less than $50,000. The spousal participation rule has been eliminated, unless your adjusted gross income is more than $150,000. With the Roth IRA, there is no restriction regarding your participation in an employment-based retirement plan such as a pension, profit-sharing, 401(k), or some other program set up by the employer for the benefit of its employees. Thus, in certain households, you may find the spouse participating in an employment-based retirement plan contributing to a Roth IRA while the nonworking spouse makes a deductible contribution to a traditional IRA.

Generally, the choice between a traditional IRA and a Roth IRA boils down to tax-deferred versus tax-free. If the money in a Roth IRA grows steadily over a long period, you'll be thrilled when you can take it out without paying taxes. If you qualify to make tax-deductible contributions to a traditional IRA and choose the Roth IRA instead, you'll be giving up a tax break now for considerable tax savings down the road.

Another advantage of the Roth IRA is that there is no required minimum distribution at age 70½, unlike the traditional IRA where you are forced to make withdrawals at age 70½, whether you need the money or not. With the Roth IRA, you can even keep making contributions beyond age 70½. But because this is a book on how to finance early retirement, I won't spend much time talking about this so-called benefit. We'll assume you want to enjoy the fruits of your labor at an early age, rather than looking for ways to hoard your money forever.

It is also possible to convert a traditional IRA into a Roth IRA, but you would pay taxes on the current value of the IRA at the time of conversion. If you're thinking of converting your existing IRA to a Roth IRA, consult with an expert before doing so. There are many complex tax and investment issues that must be taken into consideration.

Fees on your IRA are extremely important. Over the years, the charges for maintaining your IRA can reduce your return by a sizable amount. If you have IRAs in several places, you may pay several fees. It might pay to consolidate your IRAs. You can do so by directly transferring the assets from one IRA to another. This direct rollover from trustee to trustee has no tax consequences. By choosing a direct rollover, your distribution is not taxed in the current year and no income tax will be withheld. However, the IRS will come knocking when you take money out of an IRA or employer plan.

INVESTING YOUR IRA MONEY

I have discussed at length various ways to invest for retirement. To take full advantage of your investments, it is important to also discuss self-directed IRAs. A self-directed IRA gives you more choice about how your money is invested. You can open up a self-directed IRA at a brokerage firm, mutual fund company, or bank.

Although you'll have many choices with a self-directed IRA, you'll be limited to only IRA qualified investments. Investment products advertised as "IRA qualified" are permitted to be part of the portfolio in your retirement account. Only certain types of investments are eligible to be held in an IRA.

Typically, most people hold traditional investments in their IRAs. An IRA can be invested in mutual funds, U.S. Treasury bonds, money market accounts, and bank certificates of deposit (CDs). You can also keep blue chip or even penny stocks, which are extremely risky, in an IRA. Penny stocks are those that trade for under $5.

Syndicated personal finance writer Linda Stern has even suggested that you can use the money in your Roth IRA to purchase a vacation or retirement home. Although you can't live in the house while it's held in the IRA, you're entitled to visit it a few weeks each year to take care of maintenance and repairs. All the rental income stays in the Roth IRA and is tax-free.

When you're ready to make the house your permanent dwelling, you take it out of the Roth IRA. Once you live in it for two years or longer, you can take advantage of the tax break that applies to the sale of your primary dwelling. As we'll discuss in Chapter 11, you can exclude up to $250,000 in capital gains if you're single and $500,000 if you're married. However, as Stern pointed out, there are many tricky tax and investment issues to deal with before considering this option.

Certain recently minted coins may also be held in an IRA. You can even keep gold, silver, platinum, and palladium bullion in IRAs established in 1998 or later. However, most financial planners would question the wisdom of putting those types of investments in an IRA. The basic concept of a retirement account is to shelter the earnings on your investments and you'll only derive capital gains from the sale of these commodities, if you're lucky.

Some investments aren't permitted to be held in an IRA. You can't hold life insurance policies or collectibles. Although antiques and stamp collections are a form of investing, they can't be kept in an IRA.

Also, be aware that if you keep all your retirement money in a bank, you might inadvertently be taking a different kind of risk. As your retirement accounts grow, you may be exceeding the $100,000 FDIC (Federal Deposit Insurance Corporation) coverage. Unless your bank is in excellent financial shape, this is a risk you should avoid. The combined amount in your Roth and traditional IRAs will only be insured up to a maximum of $100,000. For additional information, contact the FDIC at 800-934-3342 or visit the FDIC Web site at www.fdic.gov.

PREMATURE WITHDRAWAL PENALTIES

We've mentioned the magic age of 59½. It's an event that should be celebrated, not ridiculed with Grim Reaper balloons as other milestones are. The IRS, the only group feared by the Grim Reaper, permits you to take out money from your IRA at this age without the 10 percent premature withdrawal penalty. Premature withdrawal penalties are the tax code's way of saying you're too young to retire.

The party stores haven't caught on yet. There are no cards, mugs, or other novelties announcing that you've reached the magic age of 59½. There are plenty of gifts for ages 40, 50, and 60, but not 59½. And if you think a lot about early retirement, 59½ is the age to keep in mind.

There are some complex rules that apply to distributions from IRAs, 401(k)s, and other retirement savings account. If you receive a distribution prior to age 59½ and don't roll it over, you'll normally pay a 10 percent penalty on the taxable portion. Along with this premature withdrawal penalty, you may also owe income tax on the distribution.

The same legislation that created the Roth IRA made premature withdrawal less of a problem. Many new rules apply to all IRAs, not just Roth IRAs. In his book *Maximize Your IRA* (Dearborn 1998), Neil Downing, a certified financial planner and award-winning personal finance columnist, outlines the circumstances in which you won't be subject to the 10 percent penalty. They are:

- Age 59½ or older
- Disability
- Death
- Withdrawal as part of a series of substantially equal withdrawals made at least annually over your life expectancy or the life expectancy of you and your beneficiary
- Unreimbursed medical expenses that exceed 7.5 percent of your adjusted gross income
- Withdrawal for qualified higher education expenses
- Withdrawal to pay expenses as a first-time homebuyer

Downing also notes that you can escape the penalty if you're withdrawing money to pay for medical insurance premiums for yourself, your spouse, and/or your dependents. The catch is that you must be unemployed and meet certain conditions. We'll analyze this issue at length in Chapter 12 in conjunction with insurance issues associated with early retirement.

As mentioned earlier, you won't pay the 10 percent penalty if you're withdrawing money to pay for your first home or the first home of a qualified relative. If you're trying to retire early, you shouldn't be taking money out of an IRA to help pay for a child's first home. As we'll see in Chapter 13, this may be the time to look out for yourself first.

You can also avoid the premature withdrawal penalty associated with an IRA if the money is used for qualified educational expenses. Once again, think long and hard before withdrawing money to pay for your child's education. The money you'll lose for your retirement, early or otherwise, will be hard to make up. If you feel guilty about your child taking out student loans, you can help him or her pay them back at a later date. Using IRA money to pay for a child's education is going to cause you problems down the road.

All withdrawals from a Roth IRA are treated as contributions first and earnings next. As a result, no 10 percent penalty is applied to pre–59½ withdrawals until you've exceeded the amount actually contributed to the Roth IRA. Once you begin taking out earnings on those contributions before age 59½, you'll be subject to a penalty and income taxes.

Let's say you open a Roth IRA and hold the money in there for ten years. At $2,000 per year, you'll have $20,000 you can withdraw without penalty before age 59½. Unfortunately, you'll be undermining the financing of your early retirement.

As we saw in Chapter 6, there's another way to gain access to your IRA money for early retirement without a penalty. The tax code permits annuitizing your IRA. You must make substantially equal periodic withdrawals based on your life expectancy for at least five years.

According to David S. Rhine, CPA and national director of family wealth planning for BDO Seidman, LLP, there are three methods of withdrawing IRA money early. The first is the life expectancy plan. You withdraw the principal in your retirement accounts in chunks that are based on your life expectancy. If you have $600,000 and a 30-year life expectancy, you can take out $20,000 per year. However, that's not going to finance your early retirement, unless you have additional sources of income.

The problem with this plan is that it does not factor the earnings on your IRAs into the calculation. Therefore, it does not provide much in the way of annual income. The good news is that the remaining funds are growing, even though you're withdrawing $20,000 per year. You may still be earning a lot more than you're taking out.

The IRS permits you to utilize your beneficiary's life expectancy if you prefer. Because you're trying to maximize income, this may only make sense if your beneficiary is much older than you.

The second method of withdrawing money from an IRA is the amortization plan. Under this plan, you're able to take out much more each year, because you're including the return on your investment in the calculation. The calculation involves multiplying the rate of return by the number of years you're expected to live. You then calculate how much to withdraw each year, so there are no funds left at the time you're expected to die.

The third method of withdrawing money is the annuity plan. This plan uses insurance mortality tables, which assume a shorter life expectancy and a higher interest rate. Because of these factors, you're able to take out more money each year. Unfortunately, you'll need a CPA or an actuary to calculate the amount of your withdrawal.

Even though you can get at your IRA money before age 59½ without a penalty, there are risks in doing so. If retirement isn't your cup of tea and you begin working again, you must continue making withdrawals for at least five years. If you're earning a comparable salary to your previous wage, the IRA withdrawals may cause you to be in an unfavorable tax bracket and a sizable chunk of your saving could be lost in taxes.

Another negative of tapping your IRA before age 59½ is that your IRA then doesn't grow as it once did. If you're planning for retirement in stages, you will be cutting into the money that was earmarked for age 59½ and beyond. However, if your IRA is large enough, it won't make a difference.

With the amortization or annuity plan method of withdrawal, you risk running short of money. Your investments may not produce the rate of return you've expected. You also may live longer than the tables predict. At some point, you'll need to readjust the amount you're withdrawing from your IRAs.

As mentioned in Chapter 6, 403(b) plans permit periodic withdrawals at any age, as long as they're based on your life expectancy. By doing so, you can avoid the 10 percent penalty on early withdrawals. 401(k) plans don't permit that type of penalty-free withdrawal prior to age 59½, although there is a way to access the account at age 55 or older if you are separated from service. Nevertheless, you can roll over your 401(k) into an IRA and take substantially equal periodic payments.

While there are ways to access an IRA prior to age 59½, these retirement accounts are meant to finance the post–59½ stage of your retirement. Unless they've grown enormously over the years, tapping them early may cause you problems down the road. It's usually best to delay tapping tax-sheltered accounts until it's absolutely necessary.

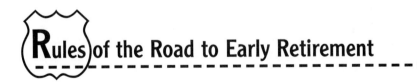

Rules of the Road to Early Retirement

▶ Take advantage of the Roth IRA. Although contributions are limited to $2,000 per year and aren't deductible, the earnings are tax-free when withdrawn as long as you're at least 59½ and the account has been open for five years.

▶ With the Roth IRA, there is no restriction regarding your participation in an employment-based retirement plan. Assuming your income isn't too high to qualify for a Roth IRA, you may participate in both.

▶ You may make a tax-deductible contribution to a traditional IRA, regardless of income, if neither you nor your spouse is covered by an employment-based retirement plan. If one of you was covered for even part of the year, income limits come into play.

▶ Usually, a nonworking spouse may make a full contribution to a Roth IRA or a traditional IRA, as long as the working spouse earns more than their combined contribution.

▶ Although there are ways to access your IRA prior to age 59½, think twice and then think some more. You'll stunt the growth of your IRAs by tapping them to pay for college expenses or a first home.

▶ You can avoid premature withdrawal penalties by making substantially equal withdrawals based on your life expectancy. Be cautious, however, because cutting into your nest egg before reaching the traditional retirement age is dangerous. These withdrawals must continue for at least five years, so you must live with your decision for a while. Normally, you're better off waiting to tap tax-sheltered accounts until you have no other source of funds.

≈ Pensions

In *Business Insurance,* an industry publication, David Strauss, the executive director of the Pension Benefit Guaranty Corporation (PBGC), tells a story about his father. His father, a meat cutter in North Dakota, retired at age 63 without a pension. He took a part-time job as a school janitor. When he retired from that job 15 years later, he received a pension for the first time. The $169 he received each month made a significant difference in his parents' lifestyle because it added an extra 20 percent to the income they received from Social Security.

From his father's experience, Strauss learned the importance of having a predictable benefit for life. The extra monthly benefit went a long way in North Dakota, which has a relatively low cost of living. The pension from the janitor job was his first defined benefit plan.

Retirement plans are structured in two ways. A 401(k) retirement savings plan is a defined contribution plan. The plan defines how much you can put away in the plan and how much the employer will match, if any. Usually, you can opt for fixed-rate investments or riskier alternatives.

The pension plan that covered Strauss' father was a defined benefit plan. Employers decide where their money will be invested. A defined benefit plan provides a specific benefit when you reach a specified age. With a defined benefit plan, the longer you stay with the company, the better your pension will be. Normally, the employer is responsible for making the required contributions to the plan so that it's funded sufficiently to make the appropriate benefits when required. The PBGC notes that "a defined benefit pension is a predictable, secure pension for life."

Periodically, you'll read about large corporations whose pension plans are underfunded. Fortunately, if a company goes under, the PBGC picks up the appropriate payments, subject to certain limits. Larger pensions won't necessarily be protected. The PBGC is a U.S. government agency.

However, the trend is moving away from defined benefit plans. According to Strauss, there has been a significant drop in the number of defined benefit plans. The PBGC now insures 43,000 defined benefit plans a huge decline from the 95,000 plans the agency insured in 1980. Most small employers do not offer defined benefit plans because of the high administrative costs and numerous government regulations. Fewer workers will be able to count on a fixed amount each month from a company pension.

The PBGC is attempting to encourage companies to offer defined benefit plans. To do this, the PBGC wants to simplify the complex rules relating to defined benefit plans. Strauss is a believer in defined benefit plans because employees are not saving enough on their own.

Some workers are taking more responsibility for funding their retirement. But while many have millions of dollars in their accounts, the average amount in a 401(k) is $29,000 and the median amount is $10,000. And that's not going to help much if it's the only money you've saved for retirement and you aren't entitled to a pension.

Some people don't even know they're entitled to a pension. In the April 27, 1998, edition of *USA Today*, the PBGC placed an ad, seeking missing pensioners. The PBGC was seeking about 5,500 people who are owed pension money. They might have worked for a company that went out of business or closed its pension plan. The agency offers a Pension Search Directory by writing to:

Pension Search
Pension Benefit Guaranty Corporation
1200 K Street, NW
Washington, DC 20005

The PBGC Web site also lets you check to see if money is owed to you. It can be found at www.pbgc.gov.

Most people are aware if they're owed a pension, but just can't figure out how it's calculated. With most pensions, your benefit depends on your earnings, your age when you begin collecting, your length of service, and the formula utilized in the plan. The formula might use an average of your pay in the last three to five years of employment.

It behooves you to understand how that pension is calculated. Otherwise, you might call it quits prematurely and blow a significant portion of the pension. According to *Fortune* magazine, the pension of a worker leaving at age 50 might be worth less than one-third of the value it would have if the individual had remained until age 55. Set up a meeting with your plan administrator and go through several retirement scenarios.

Several large companies now offer cash balance pensions. Typically, the employer puts 5 percent of the employee's pay into the individual's pension account each year. The employer also pays interest on the balance in the account. When employees leave, they may roll over the funds in the account into an IRA or a new employer's retirement plan. If you've been covered by a traditional plan and your employer switches to a cash balance pension, make sure you're not being shortchanged.

PENSION VESTING

With any plan, you must be concerned with vesting. Vesting is the amount of time you must work to earn a nonforfeitable right to your accrued benefit. Once you're fully vested, the accrued benefit is yours, even if you can't collect it at that moment in time. The plan will stipulate rules regarding when the employer's contribution will vest.

The Employee Retirement Income Security Act of 1974 (ERISA) established rules regarding pensions and other matters. The plan must comply with ERISA, which sets certain minimum standards for vesting. Your plan may provide for a different standard, as long as it's more generous than the minimum standard required by ERISA. Your summary plan description will outline the employer's vesting schedule.

Generally, there are two types of vesting schedules. There is a seven-year graded vesting schedule, which looks like the following:

Less than 3 years	0%
At least 3 but less than 4	20%
At least 4 but less than 5	40%
At least 5 but less than 6	60%
At least 6 but less than 7	80%
At least 7 years	100%

The process is called graded because vesting begins in year three and is complete in year seven.

The second type of vesting schedule is called cliff vesting. Cliff vesting is an all or nothing approach. The five-year vesting schedule stipulates that the full benefit must vest once you've worked at least five years for the employer. If you leave before five years are up, you forfeit the pension.

PENSION OPTIONS

If you will someday receive a pension pursuant to a defined benefit plan, it may not do you much good in your early retirement planning. With many plans, you can't collect until a traditional retirement age. If you do collect early, you'll probably receive much less than you would by waiting. With many plans, you can collect a lump-sum distribution of your pension plan. A lump-sum distribution is payment to the employee of the entire value of the retirement plan, instead of a series of payments.

Some experts recommend taking a lump-sum distribution and rolling it over into an IRA. They feel you'll do better by investing the money yourself. With the right investments, you may be able to make much more each month than you would in pension benefits. That logic presumes, however, that you will roll the money over into an IRA and won't just blow it on licorice.

Another argument in favor of taking a lump-sum payout of your pension is the survivorship issue. With certain plans, you may qualify for a pension after five years, but benefits for your spouse aren't guaranteed until you've been employed for a longer period. As a result, your spouse may be out of luck if you die because the pension is yours only for as long as you live.

This issue differs from the pension max dilemma that is more familiar to people. With pension max, the individual opts to take a larger monthly pension benefit. In exchange for a larger pension check, however, the spouse gives up any survivor pension. This can cause some serious problems when you die. Your spouse will have no entitlement to your pension and may run short of funds.

Many insurance companies use this situation to sell life insurance. The pitch is that you can take a larger pension benefit and still protect your spouse. To do this, you would opt for the pension benefit that provides income for your lifetime, but does not continue paying after your death. Making this choice maximizes your income. By buying a life insurance policy, there will be a death benefit for your spouse, even though he or she won't be entitled to your pension.

If you're not married or your spouse is entitled to a survivor's pension, you might want to refrain from taking a lump-sum payout. Everyone needs different types of assets to depend on. If you are scheduled to receive a fixed income for life from a defined benefit plan, even a modest one, build the rest of your investment portfolio around it. The key to reducing risk is diversification. A pension will be the conservative element of your portfolio. You can supplement it with riskier investments. A pension looks even better if it is indexed to the rate of inflation.

ERRORS IN PENSION PLANS

The U.S. Department of Labor cites these ten common causes of error in pension calculation:

1. All relevant compensation, such as commissions, bonuses, and overtime, were not included.
2. The calculation was not based on all your years of service.
3. The plan administrator used an incorrect benefit formula such as the wrong interest rate.
4. The administrator used incorrect Social Security data in the calculation.
5. Basic information, such as your birthday, was inaccurate.
6. If your company merged with another company or went out of business, there was confusion over the correct amount of benefits.
7. Assets in your account were valued improperly.
8. Your employer failed to make the required contributions on your behalf.
9. Mistakes were made in the calculations.
10. Your human resources department was not notified of changes affecting your benefits.

If you run into problems, you can call the Department of Labor at 202-219-8776 or write to the following address:

U.S. Department of Labor
Pension and Welfare Benefits Administration
Room N 5619
200 Constitution Avenue, NW
Washington, DC 20210

Hopefully, you won't have any difficulty collecting your pension. However, you should be keeping all of your records regarding how much you're entitled to and when. With companies merging daily, the rules may be changing without your knowledge.

Go to your human resources department and obtain a copy of the Summary Plan Description (SPD). The SPD contains all the rules affecting your pension. If your company merges, find out what changes are going to be made in the plan.

If you feel you're being shortchanged, you may need to contact an actuary. You might also turn to AARP, Worker Equity, 601 E Street, NW, Washington, DC 20049. Another possibility is the Pension Rights Center, 918 16th Street, NW, Suite 704, Washington, DC 20006. You can call the Pension Rights Center at 202-296-3776. They will send you the names of pension lawyers in your state.

The National Center for Retirement Benefits, Inc. in Northbrook, Illinois, charges nothing to check your pension payout. Its fees are determined on a contingency basis. The company takes 30 percent of any money recovered, and less in certain circumstances. Their phone number is 800-666-1000.

Be wary of salespeople who talk about pensions in their sales pitches. Salespeople like using the term *pension* because it sounds secure and connotes an income for life. Much like annuities, you can't outlive the income. There's no risk of the checks stopping while you're still alive. Agents for one major life insurance company sold private pension plans to customers. These private pension plans turned out to be just life insurance policies. If you've been victimized in this way, call your state's insurance commissioner.

GOING AWAY PRESENTS FROM YOUR EMPLOYER

Oxford Health Plans, a large HMO, struggled with what CNN labeled a computer systems debacle and managerial problems. As a result, the HMO ran into substantial financial problems. The CEO of Oxford, Stephen Wiggins, had fewer financial problems. For his service to the company, Wiggins received a $9 million retirement package according to documents filed with the Securities and Exchange Commission. Few readers of this book will walk away from their employment with a retirement package of $9 million. Whereas Wiggins may not have been quite ready to walk away, he did get a nice going away present.

The early retirement strategies in this book assume you will leave the workforce early out of choice. These strategies do not anticipate you receiving a package from an employer that is anxious to reduce its workforce. Aside from early retirement, the strategies in this book also are aimed at helping people achieve financial independence so their futures won't be destroyed by employers who end their careers prematurely. Although you won't necessarily be able to retire if the ax falls, you'll be able to withstand some of the financial damage.

While most people won't get a golden parachute when their job ends, Al Dunlap, CEO of Sunbeam, received a nice check when he found himself on the wrong end of his own chainsaw. Dunlap, the so-called poster boy for corporate downsizing, walked away with enough cash to retire. Nevertheless, getting fired is a devastating event. It's stressful for the person being fired and for the person who terminates the employee. A recent study, conducted at 45 hospitals across the country, found that managers double their risk of heart attack during the week after they fire someone.

If this event occurs before you're ready to retire, you face some serious problems. Your age may make it difficult to find a comparable position. During a period of unemployment, you will be draining the resources you've put aside for retirement. And after a firing or layoff, you won't be contributing to a retirement savings plan at work.

A termination may be fortuitous, if you are offered a buyout package and are close to early retirement anyway. The extra money will help you reach the actual date you planned on for early retirement. The Older Workers Benefit Protection Act mandates that employees be given at least 21 days to decide whether to give up their right to sue in exchange for a buyout package. Workers must also be given seven days to change their mind about accepting the buyout offer.

A recent U.S. Supreme Court case held that ousted workers may still sue an employer for age discrimination, even if they signed a waiver in exchange for a buyout package. For a release to be valid, employers must comply with federal disclosure requirements and the Older Workers Benefit Protection Act, which covers employees age 40 and older.

If offered a buyout or early retirement package, remember that you do have leverage. You're dealing with someone who probably feels very guilty and stressed out. You may be able to negotiate a better deal. As we'll discuss in Chapter 12, benefits are often more important than cash. You may be able to negotiate for extended health insurance coverage beyond what is required by law.

The odds of you receiving a buyout offer are becoming slimmer. For many years, you would hear tales of employers making extremely generous buyout offers. In exchange for the acceptance of a buyout offer, employers add a specified number of years to your service record and to your age. The result is a higher pension for you, because you're credited with more years of service and additional years tacked onto your age.

American Express' publication, *The Advisor*, indicates four components in an early retirement package that should be evaluated. Most companies offer:

1. Your regular pension reduced according to your current age
2. A bonus (lump sum or annual installments) that essentially makes up for the reduction in your pension
3. A bonus to compensate for the fact that you're not getting Social Security
4. Medical insurance

Just as your chances of receiving a buyout are slimmer, the days of the defined benefit plan seem to be numbered. Fewer workers will receive a pension. Pensions have been replaced by defined contribution plans, such as 401(k)s, which put the ball in the employee's court. Therefore, a buyout might be limited to a week or more of salary for each year of service. Unless you're awfully close to the time when you can retire, severance pay isn't going to go far enough.

If you aren't being forced out, think twice before agreeing to leave your job. The real danger with accepting severance packages and buyouts before you're ready to retire is the damage you're doing to your 401(k). If you accept a buyout, you'll stop contributing to your retirement savings account. Depending on how long you would have worked for that employer, you might be losing hundreds of thousands of dollars in retirement savings. You'll lose what you would have put away, along with your employer's contribution. If you go to work elsewhere, you'll probably be required to wait to join that company's 401(k) retirement savings plan.

In 1992, the company I worked for was trying to scale back its workforce. The company offered a voluntary separation package to employees in certain departments. I think I ran over five people on my way to sign up for the package. My wife's employer was in the same predicament at that time. Knowing that the company wanted to downsize, she was able to negotiate a voluntary separation package. Both of us received two weeks pay for each year of service. It wasn't a particularly generous package, but we were more than ready to call it a career.

We weren't quite ready to retire, however. At that time, we simply wanted a break from the workforce to pursue other interests. We really didn't want to take a leave of absence and return to the same field. Our employers asked us to reconsider our decisions. However, no one hugged our legs and begged us to stay.

You're really in no position to accept a buyout, unless you're ready to leap into early retirement. If you're close, a buyout can bridge the gap until you're able to live on your other assets such as retirement accounts. As we saw in Chapter 6, if you're younger than age 59½, you run the risk of a premature withdrawal penalty of 10 percent if you begin tapping your 401(k) retirement savings account. You can avoid the 10 percent penalty on the distribution from your retirement savings account if you're separated from service and are at least 55 years of age during the calendar year when the separation occurs. If it were that simple, however, a million accountants would be out of work, so talk to one.

The normal course of action is to roll over the distribution from a retirement savings account into an IRA. A rollover is a tax-free distribution to you of cash or other assets from a qualified retirement plan that you transfer to another eligible retirement plan. The rollover must be completed by the 60th day following the day on which you received the distribution.

It's usually safer to have the administrator of your old plan transfer the distribution directly to an IRA. By doing so, the plan administrator will not withhold tax from your distribution and you'll avoid the risk of missing the 60-day cutoff for rollovers.

HEALTH INSURANCE

Before you consider any buyout offer, you must be certain you're covered under a comprehensive health insurance policy. In Chapter 12, I'll discuss health insurance for early retirees. Even the healthiest individual shouldn't be without insurance.

There is a tax rule that might come into play for people leaving the workforce with a nice separation package. You may not have to pay the 10 percent penalty for withdrawing funds from an IRA prior to age 59½, as long as you're not withdrawing more than the cost of medical insurance for you, your spouse, and your dependents. These four conditions must be satisfied:

1. You lost your job.
2. You received unemployment benefits for 12 consecutive weeks.
3. You make the withdrawals either during the year you received unemployment benefits or the following year.

4. You withdraw the money no later than 60 days after becoming reemployed.

With many separation packages, you'll qualify for unemployment benefits. Therefore, you may also qualify for this tax break. Take a look at IRS Publication 590 for more details and see an accountant.

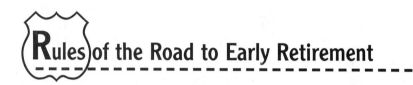

Rules of the Road to Early Retirement

▶ Start reading the materials passed out by your human resources department. If you're eligible, find out when your pension will vest. If you're close to the vesting date, think twice before changing jobs. Obtain a copy of the official plan document and a summary plan description.

▶ Find out how much of your pension you're losing by leaving at a younger age. Even if you don't draw on the pension until the normal retirement age, your monthly check is likely to be smaller. Determine if the monthly pension check levels off after a certain number of years of service. Ask if your check is offset by Social Security.

▶ Your spouse may not be entitled to a survivor's pension until you reach an employment milestone. Find out the rules. It's extremely dangerous to give away a spouse's right to a portion of your pension if you die first, even if it results in a higher monthly benefit during your lifetime.

▶ While there are advantages to taking a lump-sum distribution of your pension, a defined benefit plan is a reliable source of income that you can use to finance the post–59½ stage of retirement. Even if you're entitled to a pension, it's unlikely you'll be able to live on it. If you are scheduled to receive a fixed income for life from a defined benefit plan, even a modest one, supplement it with your other sources of income for retirement. Invest in a 401(k) retirement savings plan at work if it's offered and, if you can swing it, contribute to a Roth IRA as well. Because you can count on that check each month, you can take more chances with the other funds you've set aside for retirement.

▶ Though fewer employers are offering buyouts, it can help you accelerate your departure from the workforce. The buyout will usually make sense, if you're close to being financially ready for early retirement. The extra cash can help you through the transition period to the point when you're financially able to retire.

≈ Social Security

In an editorial cartoon, a grumpy looking man is holding a lottery ticket in one hand saying, "It's the new baby boomer Social Security card." In another cartoon, a baby boomer is kicking and shaking a vending machine symbolizing Social Security, which won't give back any of the money put in. Both cartoons express the skepticism that many are now feeling about the viability of the system.

There are many people who express concern about whether Social Security will be available for the thousands of baby boomers born between 1946 and 1964. In a little more than a decade, the first batch of baby boomers will begin retiring. As the population ages, the strain on the system will be enormous.

But even if Social Security is alive and well when you're ready to call it quits, there's another problem. You don't have to be a financial planner to realize that Social Security isn't enough to live on when you retire. Social Security will only provide a minimal portion of your retirement income if it exists in the same form decades from now. The program is meant to supplement your income from pensions, savings, and investments. For a typical worker, Social Security will replace approximately 43 percent of his or her income. It's unlikely that you'll be able to live on less than half of your current income, no matter when you retire.

According to AARP, if you made minimum-wage earnings all of your life, your Social Security benefit will replace about 59 percent of your preretirement wages. If you made the maximum wage subject to Social Security taxes, your benefit will be roughly 24 percent of your preretirement earnings. Obviously, if you earn a lot more than the maximum amount subject to Social Security taxes, your monthly benefit check will be an even smaller percentage of your wages. To visit the AARP Web site, go to www.aarp.org.

If you want to retire early, living on your Social Security check isn't an issue, because you won't be receiving one in the early years of your retirement. And I'll assume that if you're reading this book you'd like to leave the workforce before age 62. Nevertheless, Social Security benefits should be a consideration in your planning because you'll hopefully be retired for a long time.

Currently, the age at which you receive full Social Security benefits is 65. It will gradually be increased to age 67. Many politicians and economists believe that the retirement age should be raised to age 70 or higher. My guess is that none of them are reading this book or any other that deals with the subject of early retirement.

You're probably aware that your benefits will be lower if you begin collecting at age 62 instead of 65. Normally, your benefit check at age 62 will be roughly 80 percent of the amount you would collect at 65. If your official retirement age is older than 65, you'll get less than 80 percent at age 62. If you live long enough, collecting early will eventually result in your receiving less benefits during your lifetime. Even as the age when you can collect full Social Security benefits escalates, it's likely you'll still be entitled to some portion of your benefit at age 62.

Retiring before age 62 and not collecting benefits can also cause problems. Not working in the years prior to the traditional retirement age may ultimately lead to a lower Social Security check. Your Social Security benefits are based on your five highest wage years. Assuming your wages are on an upward path and aren't exceeding the maximum wages for Social Security purposes ($72,600 in 1999), ending your career prematurely may hurt you down the road even if you decide to wait until age 65 to collect. Of course, as many older workers find out, they become increasingly vulnerable to demotions as they age and their last years in the workforce may see declining wages.

Even for older workers who have saved well, early retirement may be at least five years away. For Social Security purposes, you should try to make those five years count. As we've discussed, moonlighting or working in a side business may be part of your personal plan for retiring early. If so, you might be able to bolster your Social Security earnings.

The first step is to determine how much you can count on from Social Security at age 62 versus age 65. Call the Social Security Administration at 800-772-1213 to receive a copy of your *Personal Earnings and Benefit Estimate Statement.* This report provides a listing of the earnings credited to your Social Security account. It also tells you the amount of benefits payable on those earnings. You'll find a great deal of additional information on the Social Security Administration's Web site that can be found at wwww.ssa.gov.

Make certain the figures on the report are correct. As hard as it is to believe, our government makes mistakes. It will be a great deal easier to correct those mistakes now than down the road when records may not be available. Always be certain you're being credited with every dollar of earnings so you'll get every penny you're entitled to when you start collecting.

You'll need every penny because Social Security alone isn't enough for most people to live on in retirement. People who retire before they're eligible for Social Security benefits will be used to living without them. When others retire and go from a nice paycheck to a greatly reduced income from Social Security, early retirees will already have made that leap. For those who retire before age 62, the initiation of Social Security benefits will enhance their lifestyle.

Upon reaching age 62, you can assess your situation and determine if it's time to start collecting benefits. Once you start collecting benefits, your Social Security check will supplement the money you're already receiving and improve the quality of your life. Social Security benefits will also help offset the erosion of spending power caused by inflation.

Most people aren't going to be interested in delaying receipt of Social Security benefits beyond age 65, but here's a scoop anyway. Your benefit check is increased for each month you wait beyond age 65. The delayed retirement credit is 5.5 percent per year for people reaching age 65 in 1998. If you're working part time and making a good buck, you may decide to hold off collecting Social Security to benefit from this increase.

PART-TIME WORK AND SOCIAL SECURITY

Part of your strategy for retiring early might include making money at a job you love. While money you find with your metal detector when combing the beach for treasure isn't likely to affect your Social Security check, part-time work raises issues. It's possible that the money you make will reduce your Social Security check.

For some, that trade-off makes work totally unpalatable. They paid into Social Security for decades and want every penny that's owed to them. Even if they want to work and need to work, it's not worth losing a dime of their Social Security check.

In 1999, retirees under 65 may earn up to $9,600 without any reduction in Social Security benefits. You'll lose $1 for every $2 you earn over that limit. Therefore, if you make $2,000 more than the cap, you'll lose $1,000 in Social Security benefits. This harsh penalty appears to be a way of discouraging people from collecting benefits at age 62.

If you're between ages 65 and 69, you'll be allowed a $15,500 earnings limit. The earnings limit is scheduled to rise gradually. If you earn more than that, your benefits will be reduced $1 for every $3 in earnings that are in excess of the cap. Therefore, if you earn $3,000 more than the cap, you'll lose $1,000 in benefits. After age 70, you can make as much as you want and still collect Social Security benefits.

Losing a chunk of their Social Security checks will make many people question whether it is worth working at all. Though overall you'll still come out ahead, it may not make sense to take a part-time job, especially if you're not enjoying the work. If you're working part time and making more than the cap when you reach age 62, it may be wise to wait to apply for Social Security benefits. Nevertheless, if you begin collecting at age 62, your benefits will be adjusted upward at age 65 for the months you did not receive full benefits because of part-time work.

Keep in mind that it's just earnings from a job or self-employment that will reduce your Social Security benefit. The earnings cap does not include income such as stock dividends, interest, and annuity payments. But your income from work and other sources does affect whether you'll pay taxes on your Social Security check. If your income is too steep, you'll be forced to pay taxes on a portion of your check.

If you're single and your income (adjusted gross income, plus nontaxable interest, and half of your Social Security benefits) is more than $25,000, your Social Security check will be partially taxable. Fifty percent of your Social Security benefits will be subject to income tax. If your adjusted gross income, your nontaxable interest, and half of your Social Security benefit adds up to more than $34,000, then up to 85 percent of your benefits will be taxed.

If you're married and filing a joint return, you must earn less than $32,000 to avoid tax on your Social Security check. If your income (adjusted gross income, plus nontaxable interest, and half of your Social Security benefits) is between $32,000 and $44,000, 50 percent of your Social Security benefit will be taxable. If you earn more than $44,000, up to 85 percent of your benefits will be taxable.

The formula is quite complicated, so see an accountant, if necessary. There are some quirks in the law that may surprise you. Your income for determining this tax includes tax-exempt

bonds. In addition, even if you are the only one receiving Social Security benefits, your spouse's income must be included
in the calculation.

Even without working, your Social Security benefit might
be taxed. But if part-time work pushes you over the income tax
limit, it may be a disincentive to work. Unless you're paid well
for part-time work, it may not be cost effective to hold a job.
But for those who want to retire early and don't have to worry
about Social Security yet, part-time work may be exactly what
they need.

Rules of the Road to Early Retirement

▶ Social Security benefits will help secure the second stage of your retirement that begins after age 59½. If you start collecting Social Security
benefits at age 62, your check will be approximately 80 percent of what
you would receive by waiting until age 65. As the official retirement age
increases, that percentage may be reduced.

▶ Even if you don't retire early, Social Security is only going to provide a
portion of the money you need. While Social Security will be around in
some form when it's time to retire, you'd better plan on supplementing it
with investment income or part-time wages.

▶ Part-time work can adversely affect your Social Security check. Until you
reach age 70, there are limits on how much you can earn without reducing your Social Security benefit. Furthermore, if your income is too high,
your Social Security check will be taxed to some degree.

▶ If your income is above the ceiling, whether from part-time work or not,
your Social Security benefits will be taxable.

≈ Working Less and Enjoying It More

On the old television series *The Fugitive*, Dr. Richard Kimble was wrongfully accused of killing his wife. He roamed from town to town, switching jobs while searching for the one-armed man who killed his wife. In each episode, you'd find Dr. Kimble helping out on a ranch or working at a carnival to subsidize his search for the killer. He managed to make ends meet and pay for hair dye, despite working at low-paying jobs.

For those who hope to retire early, part-time work may be necessary to make ends meet. Even for people who aren't retiring early, work is part of the picture. A recent AARP survey found that 80 percent of people polled intend to keep working after retirement.

The AARP survey confirmed the findings of an earlier poll commissioned by the Del Webb Corporation. That survey found that two-thirds of baby boomers participating in the poll plan to work at least part time after retirement. The Del Webb Corporation, builder of communities for people age 55 and older, is seeing prospective buyers who want homes with space for offices for home-based businesses.

While some baby boomers will seek part-time work to keep busy, others will work out of need. To retire early, you may need to subsidize your income with a part-time job. The ideal part-time job is one that pays a decent wage and allows you to work in a field that excites you. Part-time work sometimes makes the adjustment to retirement easier.

The best part-time job for me was as associate producer of a national series on public television dealing with personal finance and investment issues. Along with interviewing people who had questions about financial planning, I booked guests for the program who were experts in the field. I got to work in television and make a nice buck in the process.

But even if you find the ideal part-time job, don't forget that nothing lasts forever. After a successful season, it appeared the program would be produced every winter in Miami for at least three years. The situation was ideal for me, because my wife and I wanted to spend winters in south Florida and summers in Pittsburgh. Unfortunately, the series lasted only one season.

Nothing lasts forever, especially in the world of television. Similarly, if the ideal part-time job appears, you can't rely on it for the indefinite future. Worse yet, good part-time jobs are sometimes harder to find than full-time employment, unless you have skills that are very much in demand.

I held one other part-time job that was almost as satisfying. Each month, I would analyze cases for a legal newsletter. When I didn't feel like doing research on the computer in our house, I would make a trip to the law library in Fort Lauderdale. After a few hours of research, I'd walk over the bridge past the boats on the inland waterway and occasionally see a manatee. It was a perfect part-time job until the newsletter publisher sold the publication.

Whether their goal is making money or keeping busy, some people want to keep working until they lose the ability to do so. A 75-year-old man I know loved working part time. The man called a relative one day and was very depressed. Near tears, he reported that he had lost his job. Having watched downsizing among people with decades left in the workforce, it was sad watching an elderly man go through the same pain. Even though his financial needs may not have been as great as a younger person's, the 75-year-old was every bit as upset upon losing his job.

While my wife and I found perfect part-time jobs at various times, others weren't a good fit. At first, our plan was to find part-time jobs with little pressure or responsibility in fun environments. When a country club in Boca Raton held a job fair, we attended. Surrounded by hundreds of other job seekers in a large room, we worked on applications. We both reached the section on references and looked at each other. We envisioned our friends getting a call asking about our ability to handle the job as towel boy or cabana girl.

All people who earn an honest living deserve to be respected. Their jobs are as important and meaningful as anyone's. Nevertheless, these positions did not fit the image we had of ourselves at that point in time. We both worked hard at menial jobs during high school and college and believed our talents could be used better elsewhere.

We also saw quickly that low-level jobs are every bit as aggravating and difficult as better paying ones. A job at Borders book store looked attractive until we saw an employee being berated at the cash register by customers. Minimum wage does not necessarily mean minimal aggravation. We decided that if we were going to take grief from other people in the course of our employment, we should at least be well compensated for doing so.

At a Peppridge Farm outlet store, an older employee rolled his eyes as a customer questioned the prices on each item. After she left, he explained that the prices were clearly marked but some customers try to substitute one item for another. The clerk complained how aggravating it was to work there because the customers can be so difficult. Fortunately, the man explained, he only had to work there a few days per week to supplement his retirement income.

If you're planning on a part-time job to help subsidize early retirement, keep in mind that it isn't so easy to find a fun part-time job that won't be stressful or aggravating. When push comes to shove, you may not like a job for which you're overqualified or one that seems beneath you. Don't underestimate how difficult it is to go from giving the orders at a company to being at the bottom of the food chain. You might not enjoy being the lowest-paid person at your new place of employment.

Recognize, too, that some employers are reluctant to hire a long-in-the-tooth applicant for a low-paying job. They may fear that you'll quickly realize you're not suited for the position. And that just might be the case. It's not easy working at the same part-time job that's also perfect for a junior in high school.

Maybe the ideal job for you will pay a decent wage and come with travel benefits. One retiree I know works part time for a travel agent and gets some great deals on trips. Perhaps, working for a hotel chain will get you discount lodging in other areas.

If you plan to travel during your retirement, you'll need a part-time job with flexibility. Where you're working now, you probably find it hard to get away on vacation. The last thing you need is a part-time job in retirement that restricts your freedom. Establish the ground rules up front with the potential employer. Hopefully, you won't be desperate enough to accept any terms that are offered.

Some people are able to work from anywhere. They can e-mail their work to their employer from wherever they happen to be. If nothing else, hopefully a part-time job will be right in your neighborhood and won't require a lengthy commute. And unless you're working as a night watchman, the job shouldn't keep you up at night.

OPENING YOUR OWN BUSINESS

Retirement is a time when many plan to open a business, whether it's just to keep busy or make money. A writer for the *Sun-Sentinel* recently wrote about retirees who bought or opened their own businesses. One couple interviewed opened a gift shop near the beach. The husband, a former lawyer, seemed sorry they invested money in a gift shop rather than the stock market. His spouse enjoys bantering with customers but never expected to be putting in 12-hour days at this point in her life.

Coincidentally, a week before the article was published, we stopped in that gift shop on our way to the beach. Although the owner was extremely congenial, she also seemed aggravated. A young boy, shopping with his parents, came close to knocking over several items from the shelves. On two occasions, the store owner mentioned to the boy's father that an accident was about to happen, but he didn't seem to care. After several near misses, we became aggravated on her behalf and left before a fragile souvenir bit the dust.

This particular couple hopes to build the business up, sell it, and retire again. Others have found a sense of purpose in opening a business instead of retiring. A common problem, however, is the number of hours it takes to run your own business. Instead of working one job, you're handling every position including accountant, salesperson, administrator, and janitor. Unfortunately, the part-time businesses that bring in thousands of dollars for a few hours work exist only in infomercials.

Another couple quit their day jobs to open a craft business. They hoped to make the crafts during the winter and sell them during the summer. They bought a trailer to travel in to craft shows across the country. After a few months, they grew weary of that lifestyle.

As we discussed with part-time employment, opening your own business is attractive if you're doing it to keep busy and make some extra money. However, it can undermine your early retirement if you're depending on the money to live, or worse yet, if you invest a great deal of your savings to open it. Businesses can be like the house in the movie *The Money Pit*. You can keep plowing cash in and never manage to make any headway.

If your retirement is fully funded, it is extremely dangerous to use a large chunk of that money to start a business. Even if you buy a franchise that has a strong track record, you're taking a big chance. From time to time, you'll see even the most successful franchises fail.

A part-time business that requires very little capital to open is probably the best option for an early retiree who wants to dabble. Perhaps you can consult in your specialty. You'll get some great tax benefits. Some of your travel may be tax deductible. And as I'll discuss in Chapter 12, there is a tax deduction for health insurance premiums paid under certain circumstances.

A great strategy is to start your part-time business several years prior to retirement. You'll find out if the business has money-making potential. If you do make money at it, open up a Simplified Employee Pension (SEP) plan as discussed in Chapter 6. You'll then have another tax-sheltered retirement savings plan to increase the amount you're putting away.

Home-based businesses are the dreams of many. You can enjoy certain tax breaks, and commuting from your bedroom to the den keeps your car expenses low. Normally, there is very little capital invested, aside from a computer that you will probably buy anyway. If you can make a little money and enjoy your work, it's ideal for the early retiree.

As you're looking for the ideal part-time job, don't succumb to work-at-home schemes. In the Consumer Affairs Division of Broward County, Florida, complaints about work-at-home scams are frequent, ranking second behind problems involving unsatisfactory home improvement services. Ignore the ads for jobs stuffing envelopes at home and other potential scams.

Some people want to trade stocks for extra income. They sit in front of a personal computer in their home and trade stocks on the Internet. They pour through investment magazines, looking for the right stocks to buy and sell. For most of us, however, there is too much risk and pressure associated with that money-making endeavor. And when the market hits a slump, the activity isn't nearly as fun or as profitable.

Maybe, you can consult for your former employer or work part time. Some companies encourage their retirees to come back to work on a part-time basis so they can take advantage of their experience. Make sure that returning part time doesn't affect your pension and doesn't leave you feeling like you never retired.

USING PART-TIME WORK TO MOVE UP
YOUR EARLY RETIREMENT DATE

Ideally, you won't be as dependent on your part-time job as you are on your current one. Hopefully, the money you earn will be used to enhance your lifestyle rather than put bread on the table. Similarly, the primary purpose of a part-time business should be enjoyment, not to pay your bills. In a best-case scenario, you're working because you want to, not because you can't get by otherwise.

If you are willing to work part time as a trade-off for early retirement, you can accelerate your date of departure from the traditional workforce. If you're willing to take a part-time position and you can find the right one, you won't need such a big nest egg before jumping ship from your current job. Let's say you've got a $300,000 nest egg. That amount will generate $24,000 each year, assuming an 8 percent rate of return. And that's without tapping the principal.

If you need $40,000 per year before taxes to live on, you're only a part-time job away from early retirement. And if there are two adults in your family working part time, you might need to draw even less from your nest egg. In any event, working part time may be a much more pleasant option than building a bigger nest egg over the next decade. As we've stressed before, if early retirement for you means not working at all, there are other roads to take to reach that goal.

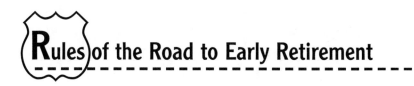

Rules of the Road to Early Retirement

▶ Start looking early for that ideal part-time job. If you plan to move to a different area, check the Internet or start subscribing to the local paper and hunting for jobs. Look up the major employers in the area and see what opportunities are available. You might even base your choice of where to retire around where the work is.

▶ When you're a year or two away from retirement, start sending résumés, even if you're not ready to move. You might find that you're not as marketable as you think and there's no particular need for your skills.

▶ Explore opportunities for part-time work at your present place of employment. Make certain it won't affect your pension or other benefits.

▶ A part-time job or small business can bring in money and help you avoid the psychological problems that sometimes accompany retirement.

▶ If you want to turn a hobby into a business, increase your level of activity prior to retiring. You might find that the odds of making money are small or that you don't enjoy it as much when you're trying to make money. If you are making money, open a SEP account to add to the money you're saving for retirement.

11

~

~ Retiring at Home or Away from Home

As we discussed in Chapter 6, you can be rich on paper and still not have enough money to retire early. Having funds in tax-sheltered retirement accounts is a lot like having money in a bank vault that opens automatically at a certain time. And that time is age 59½, unless you're willing to pay a whole lot of penalties that will undermine your ability to retire anyway. Another possibility is taking substantially equal periodic payments from your individual retirement account (IRA), but that may not produce enough money to live on and may undermine yours savings for the second stage of your retirement.

We've looked at ways to build a nest egg for use before age 59½. If those strategies don't work for you, the key to building your nest egg may be the nest you come home to every day after work. Unfortunately, to get the cash you need you might have to put a For Sale sign in front of it.

NEW TAX RULES AFFECTING THE SALE
OF YOUR PRIMARY DWELLING

A key tax break created by the Taxpayer Relief Act of 1997 is the capital gains exclusion on the sale of your primary residence. Even if you've been a pretty bad saver over the years, you may be sitting on a cash cow that can subsidize your early retirement. By selling your house, you can use the equity as a bridge to the age when you can start withdrawing from a 401(k) retirement savings account or an IRA.

The new law eliminates the 55 or older age requirement that previous existed. At any age, you can take advantage of the tax break on the sale of your primary dwelling. The new tax rule is a gift for anyone who owns a home. Previously, homeowners were required to buy a home of equal or greater value in order to avoid paying taxes on the profits from the sale of their house.

A married couple is now permitted to make a profit of up to $500,000 from the sale of a primary residence after May 6, 1997. The exclusion for single people is $250,000. And it's not just a once-in-a-lifetime tax break as it was previously. You can take advantage of the tax break every two years, if you're lucky enough to keep making money on the sale of your primary residence. The new $500,000 exemption does not apply to the sale of vacation homes, second homes, and rental properties.

If you're married and make more than $500,000 on the sale of your primary residence, you'll be taxed at a lower capital gains rate as we mentioned earlier. Instead of paying 28 percent under the old rules, you'll pay only 20 percent tax on the portion of the gain that is over and above $500,000.

To be eligible for the enormous tax break on the sale of your house, the home must have been used as your principal residence for at least two of the five years before the sale. A principal residence is defined as a single-family home, house trailer, mobile home, houseboat, condominium, cooperative apartment, duplex, row house, or even a boat. If it's a boat, it must contain facilities for cooking, sleeping, and sanitation.

There are some exceptions to the rules, so check with an accountant before giving up on utilizing the tax break. You may still qualify for a partial exclusion if the sale of your home was prompted by a job relocation, a health problem, or some unforeseen circumstance.

Anyone who's taken a home office deduction may run into a problem. If you've depreciated the house for business purposes, there are special rules that apply. It may limit the amount of capital gains you can exclude.

Aside from selling your house and living on the capital gains, the new tax rules may even give you a different way to finance your early retirement. If you are handy and a good judge of real estate, you might be able to make some money by buying a home and fixing it up. If it's been your primary dwelling for at least two years, you can take advantage of the tax break again.

It's easy to spot the flaws in this plan. First, you may have little if any equity in your home. Owning a home is no guarantee that you'll make money. In a different era, home prices escalated regularly. Even if you picked a lemon of a house, you normally made a few bucks. Today, however, real estate prices continue to stagnate in many areas.

The second flaw in this plan is that you still need a place to live and most people are content in the home they have now. Therefore, even if you can sell the house at an enormous profit, you may not want to. As I've stressed so often throughout this book, not every element of my strategy will work for everyone. If you have no desire to move to another area of the country after retiring, or you love your house too much to leave, selling it shouldn't even be a consideration.

If you have been fortunate in your home investment and the prices of similar homes in your area have skyrocketed, you stand to make a great deal of money, even after paying off the mortgage. If you're willing to trade down to a smaller house, you will have a considerable amount of cash to keep you afloat until you're eligible to draw from your retirement accounts without penalty.

Prior to the passage of the new tax law, this option wasn't available. To avoid paying the capital gains tax on your profits, you were forced to trade up to a primary residence of equal or greater value. Therefore, if you sold your house for a bundle, you were required to take your bundle and put it in another house. Under the old law, you could only escape the capital gains tax by utilizing the once-in-a-lifetime exclusion. The maximum exclusion was $125,000 and you had to be 55 or older. The new law has no age limitation and the ceiling on the amount that can be excluded has been raised significantly.

Even if your house hasn't gone up drastically in price, you'll still take away a considerable amount of cash if you've made strides toward paying off your mortgage. If you've paid down your mortgage and your house has gone up in value, you'll probably have much of the cash you'll need to make a go of it until you're eligible to draw from your retirement accounts.

However, many people want to remain in their current homes during retirement. A Westchester County, New York, woman loves her house which is now worth approximately $700,000. But she worries about the $12,000 in property taxes. She fears that those property taxes will make the house unaffordable in retirement.

Unfortunately, retirement brings forth painful decisions like whether to sell your house. Selling the house you've lived in for years is difficult, no matter how old you are. Many people only become comfortable with the prospect of selling when they realize how difficult it is to do work around the house like cutting the lawn and shoveling snow. Or maybe their children have moved out and the house is too big for them.

If you retire at a younger age, you may not be ready to give up your home. In fact, retirement may be your first chance to truly enjoy your home. As it is now, you leave early in the morning for work and return late at night. You never really get to enjoy the asset you've worked so hard to acquire. Ironically, once you're through working, the home may become too much of a financial burden.

As we've seen before, planning for retirement involves setting priorities. Hopefully, you won't have to continue working in order to stay in the house you love. Instead, you can utilize one or more of the other strategies for retiring early. On the other hand, if you're not attached to the house, your home may provide the cash you need to retire early. You can use the proceeds of the sale of your house to fund the transitional period until you're able to tap your retirement accounts at age 59½.

If you can part with your present home but want to remain in the same geographic area, consider moving further away from the city where you work. Often, outlying communities will be less expensive. Because you won't be commuting every day, proximity to your workplace isn't as important. In addition, in certain parts of the country, you can move to a different county and pay far less in property taxes. And you'll still be close to family, friends, and your favorite sports teams.

WHERE TO LIVE THE EARLY RETIREMENT DREAM

If you plan to go elsewhere in retirement or buy a second home, you have to decide where that will be. In one of the last episodes of *Seinfeld,* Kramer retires to south Florida. His coffee table book, a book that turns into a coffee table, is optioned for a movie. Flush with cash and tired of the grind, Kramer moves next door to Jerry's parents in Del Boca Vista. An exasperated Jerry tells him, "You can't live here. This is where people come to die."

For a while, Kramer lives the good life in the retirement community. He plays ping pong with a vengeance. He dances with every elderly woman in the development until an ambulance whisks more than one woman away. Then Jerry's father convinces him to run for president of the condo association. Kramer seems to be a shoe-in until he's caught barefoot in the clubhouse, a clear violation of the rules. Despite their efforts at damage control, Kramer loses the election after the article about his heinous act appears in the "Boca Breeze," the condo newspaper. Soon thereafter, Kramer comes out of retirement and returns to New York.

If you've watched any of the *Seinfeld* episodes in which Jerry visits his parents in south Florida, you might have a negative view of condominium living. But just as New Yorkers sometimes have a negative view of Florida, Floridians have a negative view of New York. A viewer writes to a Florida television columnist to ask about *NYPD Blue*. He wanted to know why the detectives live in run-down slum-like buildings. The columnist bristles at the description of apartments in New York and writes:

> I would quibble with your description of the apartment houses in which the detectives live. Their buildings resemble those in which most New Yorkers who struggle paycheck to paycheck live; buildings like those in which I lived until I had the good sense to move to Florida. They are not palaces, but they are not slums. If you want to live in the city, you compromise. A friend who recently moved to New York is paying $1,875 a month for a 500-square-foot flat in Manhattan—and he thinks he got a deal.

At $1,875 per month, retiring in New York won't be easy but other areas make it look inexpensive by comparison. *USA Today* reported that a woman with a $2 to $3 million house fund was looking for a home in Aspen, Colorado. After a few hours of house hunting, she cried. The woman learned it would take over $6 million to buy her dream home.

A real estate agent in that area was selling a new three-bedroom house for $1,699,000. The home was 2,525 square feet. Of course, it did include Red Mountain views. According to one agent, for $1.5 million you might only expect a small, undistinguished home in the unfashionable part of town or a nothing-out-of-the-ordinary condo.

Not surprisingly, Aspen has been named the most expensive place in the country to live. *Worth* magazine places the median home price at $1,512,000. While Aspen heads the list of expensive places to live, it also includes Palm Beach, Florida, Greenwich, Connecticut, and LaJolla, California.

Parade magazine described more affordable dream locations in its March 15, 1998, issue. In Kailua-Kona, Hawaii, the average condo is $55,000. A long plane ride away in Bartlesville, Oklahoma, houses cost between $65,000 and $80,000. A two-bedroom apartment rents for about $350 per month. The town offers many cultural activities.

Coldwell Banker has developed a relocation price index for almost 300 areas in the United States. It can be used to determine how much it would cost to buy a home similar to the one you have now. The guide can be obtained by calling 888-574-7653. Using the guide, you'll see that an $800,000 house in Beverly Hills might only cost $100,000 in Killeen, Texas.

The bottom line is that you don't have to trade down to cut the cost of your lifestyle. The price comparison index looks at similar homes in different areas of the country. The index compares single-family dwellings that are approximately 2,200 square feet. The homes have four bedrooms, 2½ baths, and a two-car garage. If you're willing to scale down the size of your home, your costs will be even lower.

HOME PRICE COMPARISON INDEX

To use the index, multiply the market value of your home by the index number of the city where you plan to move. Divide that figure by the index number of the market where your current home is located.

City/State	1998 Average Sales Price	1998 Index Number	City/State	1998 Average Sales Price	1998 Index Number
ALABAMA			**ARKANSAS**		
Huntsville	$136,268	61	Fayetteville	$137,844	62
Mobile	155,285	70	Fort Smith	121,227	55
Montgomery	174,767	79	Little Rock	142,909	64
ALASKA			**CALIFORNIA**		
Anchorage	223,293	101	**Northern California:**		
Fairbanks	191,305	86	Bakersfield	182,231	82
Juneau	242,412	109	Chico	204,125	92
			Davis	230,875	104
ARIZONA			Fremont	448,308	202
Mesa	154,362	70	Fresno	186,371	84
Phoenix	216,890	98	Modesto	184,690	83
Scottsdale	218,347	98	Monterey		
Tempe	164,364	74	Peninsula	455,400	205
Tucson	181,372	82			*(continued)*

City/State	1998 Average Sales Price	1998 Index Number	City/State	1998 Average Sales Price	1998 Index Number
Oakland/Montclair	396,558	179	Westport	454,660	205
Pleasanton	400,479	181	Greater Hartford	245,234	111
Sacramento	224,969	101	New London	207,568	94
San Francisco	670,824	303			
San Jose	445,611	201	**DISTRICT OF COLUMBIA**		
San Mateo	578,450	261	Metro Washington	273,279	123
San Rafael	439,875	198			
Santa Maria	221,663	100	**FLORIDA**		
Walnut Creek	370,108	167	Boca Raton	189,288	85
Southern California:			Clearwater	175,592	79
Los Angeles County:			Coral Springs/		
Agoura Hills	327,275	148	Ft. Lauderdale	159,912	72
Beverly Hills	812,225	366	Jacksonville	154,455	70
Brentwood	634,940	286	Miami	178,474	80
Hollywood Hills	334,669	151	Naples	185,431	84
Long Beach	336,550	152	Orlando	150,716	68
Palos Verdes	481,505	217	Sarasota	217,989	98
Pasadena	446,790	202	Tallahassee	149,662	68
Santa Clarita	252,810	114	Tampa	152,157	69
Torrance	330,623	149	West Palm Beach	149,387	67
Orange County:					
Irvine	268,533	121	**GEORGIA**		
Mission Viejo	276,660	125	Athens	155,154	70
Newport Beach	530,332	239	Atlanta	190,252	86
Yorba Linda	248,835	112	Columbus	206,438	93
Riverside County:			Dalton	219,338	99
Palm Springs	186,825	84	Savannah	242,775	110
Riverside	174,264	79			
Ontario	150,000	68	**HAWAII**		
San Diego County:			Honolulu	374,100	169
Encinitas	281,430	127			
La Jolla	545,900	246	**IDAHO**		
San Diego	236,556	107	Boise	167,044	75
COLORADO			**ILLINOIS**		
Colorado Springs	181,388	82	Aurora	203,238	92
Denver	196,464	89	Barrington	326,553	147
Fort Collins	210,255	95	Bloomington	154,705	70
			Carol Stream	232,689	105
			Champaign	144,784	65
CONNECTICUT			Chicago/		
New York Metropolitan Area:			Lincoln Park	473,265	213
Greater Danbury	246,569	111	Deerfield	283,170	128
Darien	522,518	236	Elgin	183,495	83
Greenwich	694,161	313	Flossmoor	241,700	109
Litchfield County	216,323	98	Joliet	158,807	72
Norwalk	328,104	148	Naperville	220,331	99
New Haven	194,088	88	Orland Park	256,068	115
Ridgefield	382,480	173	Peoria	186,151	84
Stamford	358,679	162			

City/State	1998 Average Sales Price	1998 Index Number	City/State	1998 Average Sales Price	1998 Index Number
Rockford	163,539	74	Howard County	247,095	111
Schaumburg	232,031	105	Montgomery		
Springfield	145,108	65	County	251,897	114
INDIANA			**MASSACHUSETTS**		
Evansville	136,881	62	**Boston Area:**		
Fort Wayne	151,199	68	Acton	322,359	145
Indianapolis	161,963	73	Framingham	283,551	128
Merrillville	160,810	73	Wellesley	537,160	242
Munster	232,538	105	Barnstable/		
Schererville	203,054	92	Cape Cod	197,006	89
South Bend	143,825	65	Greater		
			Springfield	206,863	93
IOWA			Worcester	230,782	104
Cedar Rapids	180,256	81	Lexington	465,902	210
Des Moines	167,543	76			
Dubuque	164,817	74	**MICHIGAN**		
Sioux City	212,484	96	**Detroit Area:**		
			Ann Arbor	258,763	117
KANSAS			**Macomb County:**		
Kansas City:			North Macomb		
Kansas City	158,111	71	County	168,761	76
Leavenworth/			South Macomb		
Lansing	147,919	67	County	166,562	75
Topeka/Shawnee			**Oakland County:**		
County	135,618	61	Oakland County	213,048	96
Wichita/Sedgwick			**Wayne County:**		
County	163,273	74	East Wayne		
			County	233,775	105
KENTUCKY			West Wayne		
Lexington	142,052	64	County	216,594	98
Louisville	152,782	69	East Lansing	168,486	76
			Grand Rapids	198,293	89
LOUISIANA			Jackson	159,442	72
Baton Rouge	147,318	66	Midland	158,584	72
Lafayette	139,887	63	Traverse City	178,520	81
Lake Charles	165,538	75			
New Orleans	140,015	63	**MINNESOTA**		
Shreveport /			Minneapolis	217,471	98
Bossier City	178,299	80	Rochester	147,188	66
			St. Paul	181,769	82
MAINE					
Bangor	148,603	67	**MISSISSIPPI**		
Brunswick	158,868	72	Gulfport/Biloxi	153,659	69
Portland	175,495	79	Jackson	170,943	77
MARYLAND			**MISSOURI**		
Annapolis	237,029	107	Kansas City	152,026	69
Baltimore	203,819	92			*(continued)*

City/State	1998 Average Sales Price	1998 Index Number	City/State	1998 Average Sales Price	1998 Index Number
St. Louis	162,912	73	**NEW YORK**		
Springfield	127,499	58	Albany	171,746	77
			Binghamton	130,973	59
MONTANA			Buffalo	148,652	67
Billings	139,874	63	Rochester/South-		
Great Falls	184,750	83	east Suburbs	191,743	86
			Syracuse	154,266	70
NEBRASKA			**New York Metropolitan Area:**		
Lincoln	148,580	67	**Queens:**		
			Queens North		
NEVADA			Shore	382,248	172
Las Vegas	163,453	74	**Long Island:**		
Reno/Sparks	178,716	81	Nassau, N. Shore	288,411	130
			Rockland		
NEW HAMPSHIRE			County	239,000	108
Nashua	177,533	80	Suffolk, N. Shore	237,020	107
Portsmouth	237,701	107	**Westchester County:**		
			Westchester		
NEW JERSEY			County	313,933	142
New York Metropolitan Area:			Hudson River		
Bergen County	388,940	175	Valley	357,385	161
Hudson County	190,183	86			
Hunterdon County	287,205	130	**NORTH CAROLINA**		
Mercer County	304,506	137	Charlotte	168,394	76
Middlesex County	245,014	111	Fayetteville	140,140	63
Monmouth			Greensboro	176,925	80
County	200,984	91	Raleigh	171,754	77
Morris County	281,533	127	Wilmington	178,815	81
Passaic County	245,468	111	Winston-Salem	172,935	78
Somerset County	383,216	173			
Sussex County	258,896	117	**NORTH DAKOTA**		
Union County	316,670	143	Fargo	160,568	72
Warren County	207,096	93	Minot	132,617	60
Western Essex					
County	289,821	131	**OHIO**		
Southrn New Jersey:			Akron	141,048	64
Camden County	199,092	90	Canton	162,388	73
Gloucester			Cincinnati	196,749	89
County	192,869	87	Columbus	179,497	81
Salem County	164,500	74	Dayton	159,201	72
Ocean County	194,700	88	Greater Cleveland	208,960	94
Atlantic County	163,866	74	Toledo	156,342	71
Cape May					
County	162,000	73	**OKLAHOMA**		
			Oklahoma City	106,753	48
NEW MEXICO			Tulsa	118,499	53
Albuquerque	206,550	93			
Las Cruces	191,688	86	**OREGON**		
Santa Fe	217,646	98	Eugene	200,611	90

City/State	1998 Average Sales Price	1998 Index Number	City/State	1998 Average Sales Price	1998 Index Number
Portland	218,081	98	El Paso	146,858	66
Salem	186,702	84	Fort Worth	112,291	51
Medford	160,900	73	Houston	123,936	56
			Killeen	100,350	45
PENNSYLVANIA			Lubbock	118,884	54
Allentown	187,807	85	Plano	140,632	63
Harrisburg	190,663	86	San Antonio	137,050	62
Reading	145,018	65			
Phil. Mainline/			**UTAH**		
Suburb West	300,190	135	Salt Lake City	177,114	80
Pittsburgh	171,906	78	Provo	145,550	66
York	144,654	65			
Philadelphia Metro Area:			**VERMONT**		
Bucks County	214,037	97	Burlington	216,176	98
Chester County	242,016	109			
Delaware County	262,300	118	**VIRGINIA**		
Montgomery			Norfolk	142,687	64
County	187,982	85	Northern Virginia	283,339	128
Philadelphia			Richmond	147,912	67
County	219,342	99			
			WASHINGTON		
RHODE ISLAND			Bellevue	299,886	135
Providence	201,876	91	Seattle	248,520	112
			Spokane	184,196	83
SOUTH CAROLINA			Tacoma	166,680	75
Charleston	137,272	62	Vancouver	198,653	90
Columbia	145,355	66	Tri-Cities	192,404	87
Greenville	163,013	74			
			WEST VIRGINIA		
SOUTH DAKOTA			Charleston	127,159	57
Rapid City	118,714	54	Teas Valley/Scott		
Sioux Falls	164,823	74	Depot/Milton	130,082	59
TENNESSEE			**WISCONSIN**		
Chattanooga	151,436	68	Fox Cities	161,583	73
Knoxville	137,125	62	Green Bay	155,404	70
Memphis	142,511	64	Madison	198,390	89
Nashville	168,630	76	Menomonee Falls	190,231	86
			Milwaukee	200,371	90
TEXAS					
Amarillo	138,056	62	**WYOMING**		
Arlington	135,437	61	Cheyenne	188,278	85
Austin	186,226	84			
Bryan-			**PUERTO RICO**		
College Station	134,336	61	San Juan	189,520	85
Dallas	154,248	70			

SOURCE: Coldwell Banker

Location, location, location has always been the rule that drives the sale of real estate. On a smaller scale, you'll pay extra for a lake or golf course view in most developments. A dazzling view of the ocean will jack up the price of that dream condo you've been saving for. Generally, if you're willing to drive to the beach instead of walking, you'll pay less.

Once again, these are issues you must resolve as you attempt to retire early. If looking out your window every day and seeing a great view enhances your quality of life, it's going to be worth the extra money. But if it causes you to delay the time when you'll retire, it may not be worth the extra money. You must also decide if you'll sacrifice square footage or other features for a view.

When my wife and I were shopping for our first home in south Florida, we were convinced we wanted to see the ocean out our window. After looking at some tiny condos in very old buildings, we reevaluated our priorities because there was no garage for our car and we would have to store our bicycles in the apartment. We ended up buying a coach home in a country club community that was a few miles from the beach. A golf course view was $20,000 extra, so we skipped those units. Every night, however, we walked the golf course and didn't feel cheated out of the view. We also enjoyed having a garage, although it was no thrill having neighbors who parked in our driveway when they thought we had gone north for the season.

Retiring out of the country is another option that some people are willing to consider. Paul Terhorst, author of *Cashing In on the American Dream: How to Retire at 35* (Bantam), lived in a $20,000 one-bedroom condominium near the beach in Buenos Aires, Argentina. Towns in Costa Rica have been touted as retirement havens. You should think long and hard, however, about retiring out of the country. For most of us, the adjustment would be significant. You would be very far from family and friends. If this option is palatable, make no permanent decisions until you've sampled the lifestyle for several months.

While Jerry's parents' condo development may not be exactly right for you, a home in a beach community may be a perfect fit. But it won't necessarily be the vacation getaway you've been going to for years. Spending two weeks a year in a particular location isn't the best test of where you should live. For one thing, you've probably only been going there during vacation season. The Jersey shore or the Outer Banks are great places to visit during summer, but they may not be your cup of tea during winter. We used to think we wanted to retire in Wildwood, New Jersey, or at least have a vacation home there. However, we found that it was a ghost town before and after the vacation season. A few bone-chilling evenings walking the deserted boardwalk convinced us that we wanted to live some place warmer.

The weather may not be the only thing to consider. Your favorite restaurants may be closed during the off-season. And when they're open during the summer, the prices may be beyond your reach. The prices you were willing to pay while on vacation may be too steep for standard fare. You might have to stick to restaurants that don't rely on the tourist trade.

The perfect retirement home isn't always in a vacation spot. If tourists are the town's bread and butter, you might find yourself gouged along with them. You may be better off in an area where there's competition for your business and restaurants don't rely on just three months to make all their money. Where merchants are in competition with one another, prices remain low.

Richard Eisenberg, formerly of *Money* magazine, helped prepare the "Best Places to Retire" list. As a guest on a public television program, he pointed out that some of the best places to retire are close to college campuses. Many retirees like having a university nearby so they can take advantage of educational offerings.

It also helps to have work opportunities in the area. As I've discussed, the early retirement strategy for some people includes part-time work, and it would be nice to have more employment options than selling fudge or pork rolls on the boardwalk.

Taxes are another key element to consider when determining where to live your early retirement dream. Many people choose Florida because there are no inheritance taxes. Let's assume, however, that you're more worried about the taxes you'll pay when you're alive than after you're gone.

State income tax is important even if you're not working. In certain areas, your pensions, interest, dividends, and capital gains aren't subject to state income tax. Also, look into whether withdrawals from IRAs and 401(k)s are taxable. Georgia, for example, has a retirement income exclusion for all residents age 62 and older. The exclusion will increase to $13,000 in 1999.

Your state may impose a tax on intangibles. Intangible personal property is anything that has value because of what it represents. Intangibles are stocks, mutual funds, and other types of investments. The tax is usually a small percentage of the value of your holdings. If your assets are significant, the tax will be significant too.

If you own two homes, you'll also have some tax decisions to make. Suppose you own a home in Pennsylvania, as well as one in Florida. Florida offers a homestead exemption, which reduces the property taxes for residents. By making Florida your primary residence, you'll avoid state income taxes in Pennsylvania and pay less property taxes in Florida. But wait to buy your clothes until you're back in Pennsylvania where there's no sales tax on those items. And don't forget about the intangibles tax in Florida.

WHAT TO LOOK FOR IN A RETIREMENT HOME

Because you're retiring early, it's especially important to stick to the budget you've allocated for a house. It's easy to keep raising your offer for a house you love, and before long you'll be in a position where you'll have to work to make up the shortfall.

When buying a retirement home, also make sure you understand your full financial exposure. In some communities, the maintenance fees escalate on a regular basis. You might have to pay a special assessment for a new card room even if you don't play cards. Your wishes and your budget often take a back seat to the will of the majority.

You might also be exposed to rules and more rules. In Century Village to the west of Boca Raton, a woman turned 90 and threw herself a party in the clubhouse of her condo. It would have been a wonderful affair, except the condo rules prohibited anyone under 18 from entering the clubhouse. As a result, the woman's two great-grandchildren could not come to the party. The children, ages five and seven, sat in her apartment with their mother. The administrator explained that the condo could not make an exception for the 90-year-old woman's birthday party. After all, rules are rules and they must be universally enforced.

Such is life in many condo communities. The condo sheriffs, as they're called, seem to do nothing but look for violations of the community's many rules. They are quick to point out violations, unless enforcement of the rules would adversely affect them. If you don't like someone telling you what color your house should be painted or how many flower pots may be placed on your porch, a development with hundreds of bylaws may not be for you.

There are also problems that go hand-in-hand with living in a multifamily dwelling. If you value your privacy, you may never get used to having shared walls. Over the long haul, it may be worth investing in a single-family home.

In the November 14, 1997, issue of *The Wall Street Journal*, June Fletcher wrote that a new generation of older Americans find traditional retirement spots dull and socially isolating. According to the article, they are returning to the Snow Belt to retire. Taking note of this trend, developers like the Del Webb Corporation see a market for huge retirement communities.

A company spokesperson for Del Webb also observed that people want to remain near their workplaces. Many want to work part-time or consult for their former employer. They want to maintain relationships with colleagues. On the other hand, you may have already seen enough of your employer for a lifetime.

MORTGAGES AND HOME EQUITY LOANS

As I discussed earlier, paying off a mortgage gives most people an enormous sense of freedom. Nevertheless, paying off your mortgage may leave you short on cash for your early retirement plans. If your monthly mortgage payment is modest, it may not be wise to pay off your mortgage and deplete the funds that might otherwise be used to finance the pre–59½ stage of your retirement.

If you want to buy a second home for your retirement, you'll run into a similar dilemma. If you pay cash for the second home, you'll reduce the amount of money you have on hand for early retirement. But if you take out a mortgage, it means another payment that's due each month. You'll need to add that mortgage payment, along with the expenses of that second home, to the amount you'll need each month to live on.

Although paying off loans quickly brings peace of mind to many people, it's not always the wisest course of action. Two professors from Appalachian State University compared 15- and 30-year mortgages in the April, 1998, issue of the *Journal of Financial Planning*. Their article took the position that a 30-year mortgage is clearly the best financial choice for many homebuyers if they have access to 401(k) or 403(b) retirement savings accounts. A 30-year mortgage makes better sense if you're in a high tax bracket, buy an expensive house, and plan to keep it a long time.

In the comparison made by the professors, the homebuyer with a 30-year mortgage invested the money saved from having lower mortgage payments in a tax-deferred account, and ended up much better off than the homebuyer with a 15-year mortgage. The professors' study assumed that the buyer with lower payments will continue investing the difference. The reality, however, is that homebuyers won't always do that.

You might be thinking about borrowing from your 401(k) to buy a retirement or vacation home. If you borrow money from your 401(k) to pay for the house, the account won't likely grow as fast. In addition, when you leave your place of employment, the loan will come due.

Home equity loans may play a role in helping you retire early. One possibility is to take a home equity loan on your primary dwelling to pay for the second home. In most cases, the interest on a home equity loan is deductible. Home equity loans may also serve another purpose. They may be used to keep you afloat while you're awaiting the day when your retirement accounts can be tapped without penalty. The rates on home equity loans are currently quite reasonable. You can often find a loan with no fees or closing costs. And often, there will be no prepayment penalty.

A home equity loan may help you bridge the gap for a year or two until your retirement accounts are fully accessible without penalty. A home equity loan makes sense if you're getting a tax deduction and paying a low interest rate. You may not even want to pay it off after you turn 59½ and can access retirement accounts without a penalty. If your retirement accounts are reaping a high rate of return and those earnings are sheltered from taxes, it may not make sense to pay off a low-interest home equity loan that's deductible.

BUYING VERSUS RENTING

Buying a retirement home isn't a decision to be made overnight. When people relocate for their company, they often go to a new city and make a decision about buying a house within a week. Because the decision is made too quickly, they often regret the house or area where they've chosen to live.

As much as you may hate renting, you will usually benefit from taking six months to a year to learn enough about an area to make a rational decision. This will give you enough time to flush out the best deal on a house. It will also help you avoid problems that may result from buying your retirement house before your primary dwelling is sold.

Once you're certain about the area and the house that's right for you, take your time furnishing it. I've talked before about the trade-offs you may need to make to finance early retirement.

You may not be furnishing your house with top-of-the-line furniture. The $300 lamp you're eyeing for each nightstand in your bedroom may have to give way to the $20 lamps at Target or Wal-Mart. Or perhaps, the furniture from the house you're selling up north will fit nicely in the retirement house you're buying. Of course, I've seen too many houses in Florida with furniture busting from the seams because the owners couldn't bear to part with any pieces from the four-bedroom house they sold.

You may not be able to swing the purchase of two homes and still retire early. In addition, buying a home in some areas is no guarantee of making a profit. After real estate agent fees and closing costs, many homeowners lose money on the second home.

If you're only going to own one home, you might be better off owning in Florida, Arizona, or wherever you intend to spend a harsh winter. Otherwise, you'll pay an exorbitant amount for rent during peak season. Assuming your current residence isn't in a resort community, you can usually rent there much more cheaply than in a vacation spot where the rates are jacked up for the season. Let's say you want to split time between a city in the north and Florida. Right now, you own a home in Michigan and your dream is to spend the winter in Florida. Renting in Florida might cost $3,000 per month during peak season for even modest living arrangements. Perhaps you'd be better off owning a home in Florida and renting in Michigan. Unless you rent in a Michigan resort area, you'll spend far less to rent there than during peak tourist season in Florida. As I've discussed before, shifting your paradigms can make a world of difference in your financial situation.

RENTING YOUR VACATION HOME

Many people envision themselves retiring in a vacation home, whether it's on the slopes, at the beach, or in the woods. As I mentioned, the purchase of a second home can complicate your plans for early retirement. If you view a second dwelling as an indispensable part of your retirement plan, don't expect it to be a wonderful investment. In many areas, the prices of homes are stagnating and you may not make much money. During a bull market, your money will do much better in other investments.

Renting the second home you buy for retirement can help offset the costs until you're living there more often or make it your primary residence. Obviously, there may be hassles with a bad tenant, along with the wear and tear that comes with even the best renter. Also, make certain you're aware of the rules in your community regarding renting your home or unit. In many communities, short-term rentals are prohibited in the bylaws of the homeowners association.

If you only want to rent the house or condo for a short period of time, the tax gods look favorably upon you. When you rent a vacation property for fewer than 15 days, you don't need to report the income. The same tax break applies to your primary residence, though most people don't normally rent their home. And even though you don't need to report the income, the IRS still permits the normal deductions such as the interest on your mortgage and property taxes.

If you rent your house or condo for 15 days or more, hire an accountant because the rules are a lot more complicated. Let's assume you rent the property for at least 15 days and during the year, you use it as a vacation retreat for more than 14 days or more than 10 percent of the time it is rented to others, whichever is greater. The house will qualify as a second residence, which means you can still claim a mortgage interest deduction and use your rental expenses to offset rental income.

If you use the vacation home for less than 15 days, or less than 10 percent of the number of days it is rented to others, the tax fairy may leave some really good tax breaks under your pillow. You may qualify for up to $25,000 in net rental losses that can be deducted from your other income. To qualify, your adjusted gross income must be no more than $100,000. If your adjusted gross income doesn't exceed $150,000, you may qualify for a reduced deduction. You must also rent the vacation home for profit for more than 14 days.

In effect, if you buy a second home while you're still working and don't use it much, you may have a pretty nice tax shelter. All of the expenses you'd pay anyway such as maintenance, utilities, and insurance will become tax deductions. You'll also be able to take depreciation on the house. You'll get a tax deduction for the presumed diminishment in value, even though you've actually lost no money out of your pocket. A motor home or boat, under some circumstances, can also qualify as a second residence if it has a kitchen, bedroom, and bathroom.

The bottom line is that these deductions will be particularly helpful while you're still working toward early retirement. You'll be paying off your future retirement home while saving on your taxes. Ideally, you'll be plowing the tax savings into investment vehicles for your retirement.

And lastly, forget time shares. A time share won't be a good retirement dwelling, and it is not an investment. Time shares are not the same as owning a piece of real estate because often they have very little resale value. They are simply a way of prepaying your vacation expenses.

TRAVELING DURING EARLY RETIREMENT

Everyone has a different dream for retirement. Some are couch potatoes who don't want to travel the world. Others love living out of a suitcase and always being on the go. The type of person you are will determine the right strategy for financing your early retirement.

As I've mentioned too frequently, you won't be able to do it all. Very few people will be able to buy second homes, retire early, and travel to their heart's content. As always, there will be trade-offs.

If you plan to travel the world, having an expensive home filled with beautiful possessions may not be all that important to you. In most areas, there are opportunities available for you to create a positive cash flow in relation to your housing situation. If you own your home, look at the rental value of the dwelling. Assuming there is a market for your property as a rental unit, speak with realtors to find out how much you could rent it for each month. Although you may have to pay a professional to deal with the duties that come with being a landlord, there are offsetting benefits in the form of tax breaks.

If you rent your home during your travels, you'll need to deal with other issues. Where will you store your valuables while your house is being rented? Does your insurance cover damage done by the person renting your house? Ideally, the money you collect in rent will exceed the amount it costs you to live elsewhere. At a minimum, you won't incur the expense of having an unoccupied home while you're living or traveling elsewhere.

If you'd like to base yourself in a particular city while traveling, consider renting a small, inexpensive apartment. You can keep some things there, while you're living or vacationing elsewhere. Or perhaps a friend or relative has room for you to store a few things and doesn't mind you staying there during trips back home. Whether it's the south of France or South Beach, you will be able to retire early and still travel. However, you may not be able to live in the style to which you've become accustomed. You probably won't be frequenting the same spots the stars visit in Cannes, Monte Carlo, or even Miami Beach.

For example, Joe's Stone Crab is a legendary restaurant in Miami Beach, famous for its food, trendy location, celebrity clientele, and, as you might expect, stone crabs. According to a story from Associated Press, Joe's maître d' bought a $400,000 condominium when he retired. Some suspect that the majority of his income came from $50 to $100 tips people gave him so they could get a table without a long wait. If you're retiring early, you probably won't be slipping anyone more than a few bucks to get a table and you might not even be able to eat at Joe's Stone Crab.

But retirement isn't going to be too much fun if you can't afford to go anywhere or do anything. Throughout this book, I've tried to suggest ways to retire early while accommodating your personal preferences, quirks, hang-ups, and idiosyncrasies. Unfortunately, traveling first class and retiring early may be mutually exclusive. Unless you've saved your frequent flyer points, you probably won't be traveling first class, or at least not more than once per year.

If you can't go in the style you're used to, plan carefully to get a seat across the aisle from your travel partner. If you like the window seat, book your trip in advance, so you don't get stuck in that delightful middle seat that couldn't have been designed for anyone bigger than Tara Lipinski.

When you're retired, you can use your flexibility to get travel bargains. You can change the dates of your trip to get the best airfare. There are also great cruise rates available for those who book at the last minute or travel on a particular date. If you live near a port, you can go to the dock on the day of departure and get a great rate.

When my wife and I plan jaunts out of town where we'll need to rent a car, we work our schedule around the weekend rate that applies to rental cars. By flying in on Thursday afternoon and leaving on Monday, we'll get a far better rate than we would otherwise. The rate is normally less expensive on weekends because there are fewer business travelers renting cars.

If you're 50 or older when you retire, you'll qualify to become a member of the American Association of Retired Persons (AARP). You'll then get discounts on rental cars and hotels. The toll free number for AARP is 800-424-3410. There are similar discounts available through the American Automobile Association (AAA).

Earlier, I mentioned the Entertainment book, which offers discounts on meals and other services in your area. The same book offers discounts on hotels across the country, as well as rental cars. Once again, being flexible helps you avoid blackout periods that apply to some discounts. If you're going to spend time in one particular area, you can buy an Entertainment book for that location. The book pays for itself quickly.

Discounts are available in lots of places. As you're driving across the country, there are more perks available than just free orange juice at Florida's welcome center. As you enter most states, there are discount coupon booklets given to visitors at the Welcome Center. The coupons entitle the user to incredible discounts on lodging, meals, and recreational activities. In almost every city, you can find books and coupons available in the lobby of the place where you're staying or even in the phone book. In most areas, you'll find a local community newspaper that is frequently filled with discount offers from restaurants.

There are many people who view travel as a time to splurge and not worry about money. If travel is an important component of your early retirement, you're going to need to show some restraint. Those bills you run up now are going to hit when you're ready to take your next trip.

There are other reasons traveling can be expensive. One woman puts her cat in a kennel when she leaves on a trip. It costs $15 per day. For an extra $6 per day, they take the cat out and massage its paws. You should give careful consideration to these kinds of expenditures.

Rules of the Road to Early Retirement

▶ Take advantage of the new tax rules that permit a married couple to make a profit of up to $500,000 on the sale of their primary dwelling without paying federal income taxes. The limit for single individuals is $250,000.

▶ If you're planning to travel a great deal in retirement, owning a big home may not be as important as it once was. Furthermore, if your children have left the nest, selling that house is probably in the cards anyway. By trading down to a smaller home or moving to a similar home in a less expensive area, you can come up with extra cash to accelerate your retirement date.

▶ A vacation paradise isn't necessarily the place you want to retire. Spend a fair amount of time in the area. Consider renting a place before buying. Also research the opportunities for part-time employment in the area where you're looking to live.

▶ If you're looking at a planned community, ask about all of the restrictions. There may be dozens of rules affecting your use of the property. You might not be allowed to park an RV or a truck in the driveway. Visiting friends and relatives may be barred from using certain facilities. You may not be allowed to rent the dwelling for less than a particular length of time.

▶ If you can't part with your present home, consider renting it while you're traveling or living elsewhere. You don't have to declare the income if you rent for less than 15 days per year.

≈ Insurance Issues Affecting Early Retirees

Phil, the tavern owner on *Murphy Brown,* remarked once that nobody ever lay on their death bed wishing they'd spent more time at work. In fact, it seems that work puts too many people on their death bed prematurely. Most of us have seen coworkers leave the office with chest pains or age quickly because of the demands of work.

If your job is particularly stressful, you probably wonder what long-term damage it's doing to your health. The short-term impact of work on your health is more visible. You get run down from too many hours of work and are always sick. It seems that at every meeting someone is hacking, coughing, and breathing germs in your direction.

If south Florida is any indication, retirement won't necessarily lead to a healthier lifestyle. In the course of a day, you'll see a half dozen people with their faces and noses bandaged. Usually, something has to be removed because of too much sun, skin cancer, the effects of aging, or all of the above.

Sometimes, even activities like swimming can cause a medical problem. From April to July, swimmers in Florida have to be on the lookout for sea lice. The problem, however, is that you won't see sea lice, even when you're on the lookout for them. They're microscopic organisms that cause a horrible rash weeks after you've come in contact with them. Dermatologists outside of Florida aren't much help because they rarely run into cases of sea lice.

If you're prudent about when you go swimming and use a high sun screen, you should be a whole lot healthier after you retire. But you're still going to need health insurance. Even if you're a fitness fanatic and have no vices, the risk of illness or accident is always there. While you may be able to get by without working, you can't get by without health insurance.

Most people are dependent on their employer for more than a paycheck. For many, all of their health, life, and disability insurance needs are met by their company's employee benefit package. Even if your employer contributes only a small percentage of the cost, you're probably used to premiums being deducted from your paycheck and never appreciate how expensive the coverage is. As you wean yourself from a paycheck, you must also find alternative sources of insurance coverage.

Insurance premiums may blow your early retirement plans out of the water. Even if you can live on your savings, insurance bills may sink your plans. As you attempt to solve that problem, remember that you're looking for a long-term solution, not a temporary fix. It's also imperative that you nail down coverage before leaving your job.

Some retirees thought they had nailed down their health care benefits, but were mistaken. General Motors (GM) employees who retired between 1974 and 1988 have challenged the company's right to make cuts in their retiree health care plan. The retirees thought they were promised free lifetime health care benefits. GM, however, argued it had the right to amend the retiree health care program. Among other changes, GM imposed deductible and copayment insurance requirements.

To date, the courts have upheld GM's position in the class action suit involving 84,000 workers who retired from the auto company. According to decisions rendered to date, the automaker does have the authority to reduce health care benefits. As this book goes to print, the retirees were asking the U.S. Supreme Court to review the lower court's decision.

According to Jerry Geisel in *Business Insurance,* there is considerable litigation involving postemployment health care benefits. GM isn't alone in attempting to reduce the growing cost of providing these benefits to retired employees. Therefore, even if you're fortunate enough to receive a retirement package that includes health insurance, you may not be able to bank on a particular premium or out-of-pocket expense during your retirement years. In fact, you may not be able to bank on that policy remaining in force forever.

For the early retiree, health insurance coverage is going to be a major problem. You won't be eligible for Medicare coverage until age 65. There is, though, talk of lowering the eligibility age for Medicare because many older Americans can't find affordable health care coverage and fewer employers are offering health insurance as a benefit for retirees.

A recent study from the General Accounting Office (GAO) found that people in the 55 to 64 age group who retire early may not be able to afford comprehensive private health insurance. The GAO called this group the *near elderly,* which is enough to scare any aging baby boomer. One proposal offered by the Clinton Administration would permit the near elderly to buy into the Medicare system. Nevertheless, the premiums might be quite steep. One insurance industry group opposes the administration's proposal and has suggested tax breaks for purchasing health insurance as an alternative.

LAWS NOW ON THE BOOKS

There are tax breaks available now to help people in need of health insurance. One tax rule affecting individual retirement accounts (IRAs) will help people who don't leave their job voluntarily. You may not have to pay the 10 percent penalty for withdrawing funds from an IRA prior to age 59½, as long as you're not withdrawing more than you need for medical insurance to cover you, your spouse, and your dependents. As you might expect with any tax rule, there are restrictions on this tax break. All four of the following conditions must be satisfied:

1. You lost your job.
2. You received unemployment benefits for 12 consecutive weeks.
3. You made the withdrawals either during the year you received unemployment benefits or the following year.
4. You withdraw the money no later than 60 days after becoming reemployed.

Clearly, this tax break was not meant for the early retiree who leaves the workforce voluntarily, but there may be a few people who receive a separation package and meet the requirements. See IRS Publication 590 for more details.

Even with a tax break, health insurance isn't cheap. Depending on your age and medical history, health insurance can be an expensive proposition. Even if your employer shares the cost, it can be extremely expensive. Many companies are passing more of the costs onto employees. Even as these expenses rise, it is not unusual to find employees who stay with a job because they need the health insurance.

In recent years, legislation has been passed that protects workers who are afraid to switch jobs because of a medical condition that won't be covered under a new employer's health plan. The Health Insurance Portability and Accountability Act of 1996 limits the application of pre-existing condition exclusions.

While this act helps people who are leaving one job for another, it doesn't do much for employees who leave the workforce. Then, COBRA comes into play. COBRA is the acronym for the Consolidated Omnibus Budget Reconciliation Act of 1985. COBRA in many cases permits you to buy coverage from your former employer for 18 months or more at the group rate, plus an administrative charge.

The operative word, however, is *buy*. You'll be paying the actual cost of the coverage, which may be quite high, and you're not entitled to the employer's contribution. Worse yet, group rates aren't always cheap. Group coverage rates often escalate because some employees or their family members have major health problems. This is reflected in the premium that everyone pays. A $400 to $500 per month payment under COBRA isn't uncommon.

Unless you're extremely close to the age when Medicare coverage is available, COBRA isn't a long-range solution. When COBRA runs out, you'll find yourself looking for coverage with no guarantee that you'll find an affordable policy. If you're relatively healthy, you may be able to find a permanent individual policy through your local Blue Cross and Blue Shield at a reasonable rate. Frequently, the premium for you and your family will be less than what you paid at work. If you're willing to join an HMO or some other managed care plan, the cost may be lower than a traditional fee-for-service plan.

Your local Blue Cross and Blue Shield may have a Web site that provides information on the types of plans that are available. Blue Cross and Blue Shield of North Carolina's Web site reviews the types of plans available, as well as the physicians who participate in them. The Web address is www.bcbsnc.com.

Just as your health insurance premium always seemed to be going up at work, an individual policy will go up too. Make certain you've accounted for those potential premium increases in your budget. The cost of your policy also may rise with age. In some plans, the premium rises with each age milestone such as 40, 50, and 60.

There are other sources of health insurance aside from individual plans through your local Blue Cross and Blue Shield. You might be offered group coverage through an organization to which you belong. Once again, don't just assume that the group rate will always be better. Compare the coverage you're getting and the premium with other policies. Shop around for the best price.

If your spouse will continue working, your health insurance issues may be solved for a while. However, unless your spouse has no desire to retire, this will only be a temporary solution. If you're planning to work part time, find out if it's possible to obtain coverage through that employer. But you don't want to tie yourself to a particular place of employment simply because of the insurance it offers.

Going without health insurance is not an option for early retirees. You can, however, self-insure to a degree by taking the highest deductible you can afford. Some companies also offer excess major medical policies. These are designed to offer protection against catastrophic illnesses. They add several million dollars in extra protection to the coverage found in your primary health insurance policy. There are some people who are utilizing an excess policy as their only form of medical coverage. It's an extremely risky strategy because you may get stuck with a medical bill of $25,000 or more. Essentially, these people are self-insuring with a ceiling on how much they can lose.

Don't buy coverage that only pays for medical treatment related to accidents, or the so-called dreaded disease policies. You need a comprehensive medical policy, not just one that covers a particular disease like cancer. Although these policies are relatively inexpensive, they don't provide protection against all of the medical problems we may encounter in life.

Whichever policy you buy, find out what happens if you're out of town when a medical problem occurs. If you're living elsewhere for part of the year or traveling a lot, the odds of needing medical attention while away from home increase. Before leaving home, find out what the ground rules are for using an out-of-network provider or going to the emergency room in a different city.

Even if emergency treatment is covered, the insurance company may question whether your treatment was a genuine emergency. Some policies won't cover treatment while you're out of the country. One cruise passenger I know found he wasn't covered for an emergency evacuation from the ship to a hospital. Another problem is that the policy may cover your medical treatment while away from your residence, but you'll be reimbursed at a lesser rate. Find out who must be called to approve medical treatment and take those phone numbers with you.

When you're on Medicare, you may run into problems when traveling outside the country. As a general rule, Medicare won't pay for hospital or medical services outside the United States. In certain circumstances, Medicare will pay for care in a qualified Canadian or Mexican hospital. Some Medicare supplemental policies cover these expenses.

Whether you're on Medicare or some other form of health insurance, you may be a candidate for travel insurance, which can be costly. Along with the medical coverage included in a travel insurance policy, you may also want to consider trip cancellation insurance if you're planning a major excursion. Make sure the policy includes trip interruption protection in case you become injured or ill and your travel plans are cut short.

HEALTH INSURANCE AND THE SELF-EMPLOYED

If starting a small business is part of your early retirement strategy, you may have some other options for buying health insurance. There are group health plans offered to the self-employed that may be less expensive than you think. Check with your local chamber of commerce or a trade group to which you belong.

I've discussed starting a small part-time business as part of your early retirement strategy. Aside from the money, it might lead to a terrific tax deduction. You can deduct your health insurance premiums, if you're not covered by an employer's plan. While you can't deduct every penny, the deductible percentage of your premium is going up.

The deduction is scheduled to go up in accordance with the following timetable:

1999	60%
2002	70%
2003	100%

You might also qualify to open a Medical Savings Account (MSA). MSAs are available to employees of small businesses or the self-employed. Small businesses, as a general rule, are those with 50 or fewer employees. To be eligible, you must only be covered by a high-deductible health plan.

There are many positives to these accounts. You fund MSAs with pre-tax dollars, and no tax is due if the money is withdrawn to pay medical expenses. You can withdraw the money for any reason after age 65 without paying taxes.

With all of these benefits, it is surprising there has been very little clamor for MSAs. One reason is that the insurance industry isn't enamored with the idea of selling them. They are also not available to everyone.

Having an MSA would make it easier to deal with a health insurance policy that has a higher deductible. If you run into a medical problem, you would pay your out-of-pocket expenses with funds from the MSA. Nevertheless, all of the tax advantages in the world won't take the place of a solid health insurance policy.

AUTO INSURANCE

As I've discussed before, many trade-offs are required to reach the goal of early retirement. You might need to give up that second car. Instead of trading cars every three years, you should hold onto them a lot longer. Perhaps, when your current vehicle goes to auto heaven, you'll be purchasing a reliable used car.

Even if you're able to swing early retirement and a fleet of late-model cars, you should do your best to save money on auto insurance. When your commuting days are over, advise your auto insurance company. You should pay less for the same coverage, especially if you drove to work every day.

However, being self-employed can cause your premium to increase. Even if you never leave your home for business purposes, the insurance company may put you in a business classification that has a higher premium than for someone who is retired.

Getting older does have its advantages when it comes to car insurance. At many companies, you'll pay a lower premium if you're 55. GEICO, a major automobile insurer, advertises cheaper rates available when you reach age 50.

Before you buy a car, look at the insurance rates for that make and model. If a car is more likely to be stolen, you'll pay more to insure it. The premium will also depend on how your car performed in crash tests. In addition, your car insurance will usually be lower if the vehicle has air bags, antilock brakes, and a built-in theft system.

If you're driving older cars as part of your strategy for retiring early, consider dropping the collision coverage if they're worth very little. It might be time to raise your deductible, because you won't be driving like a maniac to get to work on time. You won't need to be out on the road at the height of rush hour and can drive when the highways are less congested. In theory, you won't have anywhere to be at a certain time and you'll drive leisurely to your destination. Promise me, though, that you won't start driving for miles in the passing lane with your turn signal on.

GETTING LIFE INSURANCE
WHILE YOU'RE GETTING A LIFE

Most employers offer life insurance to their employees at little or no charge. If you still need life insurance in retirement, there are other sources from which to buy. A group to which you belong may offer a better deal than what you're paying now. Compare the rates. You might also buy renewable term insurance at a relatively low cost. You can lock in a premium for a decade or longer. By that time, you probably won't need much life insurance.

The need for disability insurance diminishes when you no longer depend on working for an income. One prong of my strategy is to work part time to subsidize early retirement. Therefore, the need for disability insurance isn't totally eliminated.

Once again, a group or organization to which you belong may offer a relatively inexpensive disability insurance policy. Most likely, the disability insurance plan you have through your employer won't adequately cover you if something happens. You may want to start looking at policies now as a safeguard against disability.

You may even be at the age when it's time to consider a long-term care policy. After looking at long-term care policies for a while, you'll definitely feel it's time to retire.

Advice on almost every type of policy is available through your state's insurance department. If your state's insurance department doesn't have a Web site, look in the phone book under state offices for the phone number. You can also obtain valuable information about insurance from the National Association of Insurance Commissioners' (NAIC) Web site that is located at www.naic.org. The NAIC drafts model laws and regulations dealing with insurance. Your state insurance department is a member of the association.

Another valuable Web site is the Insurance News Network. It provides objective insurance information dealing with almost every type of policy. The Web address is www.insure.com. As mentioned in Chapter 5, this Web site also provides the financial rating of insurance companies.

In addition, Quotesmith, an online insurance price comparison service, offers free quotes on individual and family health insurance policies. The Web address is www.quotesmith.com. This database probably won't track the rates of all the health insurance carriers in your area. Quotesmith also provides a price comparison for other types of insurance policies.

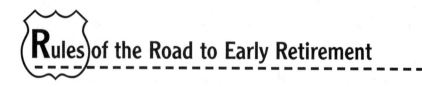

Rules of the Road to Early Retirement

▶ If you're close to Medicare age, COBRA is an option to consider. Unfortunately, with COBRA, you pay the group rate plus an administrative charge of 2 percent. Without the employer's contribution, the premium is likely to be quite expensive.

▶ Consider an individual or family plan through your local Blue Cross and Blue Shield or some other reputable health care provider. Another possibility is a group policy through an organization to which you belong. Make certain the policy is guaranteed renewable. Check with your state's insurance department for a list of health insurers offering policies in your area.

▶ Don't let your current coverage lapse until you've been approved for a solid, comprehensive policy from a reputable company. Unless you're getting health insurance through some early retirement package, find a policy while you're still working.

▶ If you're self-employed, you can deduct health insurance premiums, subject to certain restrictions. Contact your chamber of commerce, professional organizations, and trade groups to find a comprehensive policy at a better rate.

▶ There is a diminishing need for life insurance as you grow older. If there are people who depend on you for support, you'll need to replace the group life insurance you get through work. Often, you can find group coverage at rates that are the same or lower than you get through your employer.

~ How to Retire without Disowning Your Kids

In a *New York Times* article, a reporter describes a 33-year-old who holds one of the so-called glamour jobs in Manhattan. She is a salesperson at Polo Ralph Lauren and makes $8 an hour. One of the job requirements is that she purchase thousands of dollars worth of Ralph Lauren clothes. If she wears an unapproved combination of the designer's clothes, she is given a demerit and will be asked to buy a different outfit.

Because the salary is so low, many holders of these glamour jobs are subsidized by their parents. They live in the fashionable Upper East Side. Sometimes, their parents buy them an apartment. They live a lifestyle that requires an income of $50,000 to $60,000 or more, even though they earn in the neighborhood of $20,000. If you do the math, these 33-year-old *kids* require a great deal of parental subsidization.

If you can afford to buy your child an apartment on Park Avenue, the advice in this book probably won't do you much good. The $30,000 to $60,000 per year most people hope to retire on probably won't pay your real estate tax bill for the year.

More typically, people will be trying to retire early after paying for a child's tuition or wedding.

Hopefully, if you're sacrificing early retirement for your children, they demonstrate some measure of appreciation. In a letter to Ann Landers, a 28-year-old stated that she has been living with her fiancé for almost four years and they do well financially. She is planning the wedding of her dreams and wants her father to pay for it, even though he is not a wealthy man. The letter-writer proceeds to mention that her father has always been very frugal. The woman only casually mentions that he paid for her college tuition, two years in a master's program, rent, credit card debts, and other expenses, so she could travel with her friends. And what words of wisdom did she get from Ann Landers? Although Ann did recognize her as a spoiled brat, the advice columnist suggested that the woman offer to pay half of the wedding expenses and ask her father for the other half.

Some children ask little and give so much back in return. Those are the kind of children that parents want to help financially. If you aren't receiving respect and gratitude from a child you're supporting, it shouldn't be too hard to close down the bank known as Mom and Dad.

No matter how appreciative your children are, recognize that the more money you shovel toward them, the less you'll have to finance your early retirement. In a humorous commercial for a financial services firm, a parent comes looking to his son for help in retiring. While the father and son are fishing, the man suggests that the boy get a job. After all, the father says, you're already in the third grade and can read.

Unless your child's an Olympic ice skater or playing on the pro tennis circuit, don't bank on him or her for help. In most families, the dilemma is how to deal with the expenses of raising a child while saving for retirement. Even for someone who makes a nice salary, the expenses can be overwhelming. Whether it's the occasional expenditure like a prom or the everyday cost of food and clothing, parents reach into their pockets on a daily basis for their children.

One woman has a plan of her own. Her full-time business is collecting Beanie Babies. She owns 500 of them, including several that are retired. One is worth $900. The woman, whose children are ages 4 and 7, says the Beanie Babies are her children's college funds. Hopefully, she'll sell them while Beanie Baby fever is at its peak and invest the money in a mutual fund, rather than waiting a decade to unload them.

CUTTING THE CORD

It isn't easy, but you can retire early, even with children. But they can't be children who need your assistance forever. The earlier your children become self-reliant, the sooner you'll be able to retire.

In *The Millionaire Next Door,* the authors discuss patterns they found while interviewing millionaires. An important one was that their children became self-reliant at an early age. Many parents tell themselves their children are self-reliant but overlook key expenditures. They continue to pay for a child's auto or health insurance and frequently make loans that are never paid back. It's wonderful that parents are so giving, but these expenditures must end at a certain point if you want to retire early.

Many parents are used to sacrificing for their children. They stay in the workforce for much longer than necessary, so their children can have the finer things in life. There are many people who will forgo the dream of early retirement, so they can pay for college tuition, weddings, bar mitzvahs, or a million other expenditures that go hand-in-hand with raising children.

There are ways to raise children and still retire early. Is it easy? No. Furthermore, you'll probably need to work longer than someone in a similar financial situation who doesn't have children. Somehow, you must find a way to take maximum advantage of retirement savings accounts like 401(k)s and individual retirement accounts (IRAs), even though you're coping with the expense of raising children.

Perhaps that means you won't be able to indulge them as you'd like. When your children can't live without some item, make them earn it or pay part of the cost out of their own money. You'll see quickly that they can live without the purchase when Mom or Dad isn't footing the entire bill.

In a Target discount store, a child under ten years old was showing two toys to her mother. In a very analytical way, she was comparing the toys, which were quite similar, but made by different manufacturers. The little girl offered her thoughts on the pros and cons of each toy and which was the better value for the money. I'm not sure if she was spending her own money, but the young girl certainly seemed to understand the value of a dollar.

Every child needs to learn that lesson early. Children also need to learn about saving at an early age. The accounts that you start for your child at an early age need to be untouchable. When children receive cash gifts, they need to invest half or more and not touch their nest egg until it's time for college.

Notice the use of the word *invest*. In addition to getting into the habit of saving, kids need to learn about investing at an early age. Many mutual funds will waive the minimum investment, if you agree to invest a specified amount per month. In addition, dividend reinvestment plans let you accumulate shares automatically. Once you buy one share or more, the quarterly dividends can be used to purchase more stock. A child can periodically invest $25 or more and buy more shares. There are even direct purchase plans that permit you to buy that first share directly from the company without using a broker.

Many children will like the idea of investing in companies that make the products they love. Maybe owning stock in McDonald's or a toy company will tickle their fancy. It might make them get in the habit of following the stock in the newspaper. Whether it's stock of any kind or a mutual fund, children have one great advantage—time. The earnings on their investment will compound and grow significantly over time.

Most parents make incredible sacrifices for their children and give enormously of their time to raise them. If you're dreaming of retiring early, your children need to realize that you have needs too. Sometimes there will be sacrifices that they need to make, so your future will be secure. If you view that as depriving your children and the thought is unpalatable, plan on working a lot longer. It will then be you asking, "Are we there yet?" on the road to early retirement.

SMALL SACRIFICES

To save for retirement, your family may occasionally have to vacation close to home, instead of the Magic Kingdom or some other expensive tourist spot. It's not so much the price of admission or the $2 glass of milk at the International House of Pancakes that is steep. The real cost is the long-term damage to your retirement funds. If that vacation causes you to refrain from contributing to an IRA or forces you to borrow from your 401(k), you'll lose thousands of dollars down the road. While the memories of vacations last a lifetime, the damage to your nest egg can last a lifetime too.

Maybe, the expense of a prom shouldn't approach the cost of a royal wedding. When your child is ready for a car, it shouldn't be you picking up the entire tab. Junior also needs to know that the cost of owning a car isn't just the amount paid to the dealer. Your child should pay the extra insurance premiums too, along with the maintenance.

Your philosophy about raising children will have a lot to do with whether you can retire early. One couple we know wanted to put their children through college without them having to work or take out any loans. Other parents either can't swing that financially or may strongly believe that paying your own way through college builds character and makes the child more determined to finish. The latter group believes that kids are less likely to skip class and not study when the money is coming out of their own pockets.

If you have unlimited resources, there is always money available to meet your children's needs, as well as your own. If you don't, there must be a point in time when your own needs come first. The earlier that point is, the earlier you'll be able to retire.

While you're thinking about raising children, don't forget about the family pet who's almost like a member of your family. No doubt, veterinarian bills will come at an inopportune time. Leave room in your budget for those expenses. Although health insurance for pets is now available from a few companies, most people will be paying for vet bills out of their own pockets.

EDUCATION IRAS

Fortunately, you won't need to worry about paying college expenses for your family pet—just obedience school. However, you will need to be concerned with the escalating cost of higher education. Saving for a child's education and retirement at the same time is no easy feat.

The Taxpayer Relief Act of 1997 provides a vehicle for funding a child's education without too much damage to your retirement plans. The new law offers incentives for starting an education IRA for your child or children. You can contribute up to $500 per child, as long as your adjusted gross income is $150,000 or less, if filing jointly. If you're single, your adjusted gross income must be $95,000 or less. A smaller than $500 contribution is permitted if your adjusted gross income isn't more than $110,000 ($160,000 on a joint return).

You may contribute to an education IRA, even if you've already made the maximum contribution to a Roth or traditional IRA.

Like the Roth IRA, the contributions aren't deductible but the earnings grow untouched by taxes. Distributions are tax-free if used for qualified higher education expenditures. These would include tuition, fees, books, and supplies, as well as room and board. Although $500 per year isn't much money to be putting away to save for a child's education, it can grow significantly if you start early enough.

The Taxpayer Relief Act of 1997 did more than just establish the education IRA. You're now able to get at your other IRAs without penalty to pay for undergraduate or graduate school. You will, however, pay the ordinary income taxes on withdrawals made for that purpose (see the chart on the next page).

All of the money you're taking out of an IRA for educational purposes isn't subject to a penalty. Nevertheless, all of that extra income may hurt your child's chances of qualifying for financial aid during the next school year. It's also going to reduce the size of your nest egg for retirement.

Many people borrow from their 401(k) retirement savings plans at work to pay for their child's college expenses. The money you borrow isn't income, so it won't adversely affect your child's chances of receiving financial aid. Better yet, financial aid counselors don't include the cash in a 401(k) as part of your assets when calculating the aid package.

Some financial experts argue that borrowing from a 401(k) or similar plan will have a minimal impact on the growth of your 401(k) over the years because you're paying back the money to yourself with interest. The counter-argument, however, is that you may not be able to contribute to your 401(k) because of the repayment schedule on the funds you borrowed. In addition, your employer may not permit you to make contributions while a loan is outstanding.

It might make sense to opt for a home equity loan to pay for college-related expenses. You'll get a tax deduction and won't do damage to your retirement accounts. Because your income won't increase as it will for an IRA withdrawal, the financial aid office won't penalize you.

You can retire at a young age, even if you have children. It really helps to be a two-income family willing to live on a lot less than you make. One couple I know was financially able to retire in their forties. They had put away enough money for their son's education by the time he was eight. They did it without the benefit of an education IRA. It took discipline and starting early.

And if you can retire before your child starts college, think of the financial aid he or she will be eligible for.

YOUR IRA CHOICES

	ELIGIBILITY	CONTRIBUTION LIMITS	DEDUCT-IBILITY	TAX ADVANTAGES	WITHDRAWAL
ROTH	AGI: Individual $0–$110,000 MFJ $0–$160,000	Lesser of $2,000 or 100% earned income. Contribution allowed after age 70½ if still employed.	No	Tax-free earnings. Penalty-free withdrawals after 5 years.	Tax-free:[1,3] • after 5 years and • after age 59½, or • first home, or • upon death. No required distribution at age 70½.
EDUCATION	Named beneficiary less than age 18. AGI: Individual $0–$110,000 MFJ $0–$160,000	$500 per child per year.	No	Tax-free earnings. Penalty-free withdrawals for higher-education expenses.	Required when beneficiary reaches age 30. Taxable and 10% penalty.
TRADITIONAL DEDUCTIBLE	Those who are not active participants in an employer-sponsored retirement plan. Active participants may also qualify for full or partial deductions.[2]	Lesser of $2,000 or 100% earned income. Not allowed after age 70½.	Yes	Earnings grow tax deferred but are taxed upon withdrawal. Possible tax deduction of contributions.	Penalty free:[3] • after age 59½. • first home, or • higher education, or • upon death. Required distribution at age 70½.
TRADITIONAL NON-DEDUCTIBLE	Earned income under age 70½.	Lesser of $2,000 or 100% earned income. Not allowed after age 70½.	No	Earnings grow tax deferred but are taxed upon withdrawal.	Penalty free:[3] • after age 59½. • first home, or • higher education, or • upon death. Required distribution at age 70½.

Note: AGI = Adjusted Gross Income; MFJ = Married Filing Jointly

[1] Withdrawals from a Roth IRA after five years are not subject to income tax or the 10 percent premature withdrawal penalty if the participant is at least 59½, dies, is disabled, or uses up to $10,000 of the money for first-time purchase of a home. Withdrawals after five years but before age 59½ for college expenses are not subject to a 10 percent penalty tax but are taxed at ordinary tax rates. Withdrawals of contributions made at

any time are not subject to income tax or a 10 percent early withdrawal penalty. Withdrawals of earnings before five years are subject to income tax and possibly the 10 percent penalty tax. Note: Single individuals with adjusted gross income above $110,000 and couples with AGI above $160,000 cannot contribute to a Roth IRA.

[2] If covered by a retirement plan, fully deductible contributions may be possible if AGI is below $30,000 single tax payer and $50,000 married fiing jointly. In addition, reduced deductible contributions may be allowed for AGI levels between $30,000 to $40,000 single and $50,000 to $60,000 married filing jointly.

[3] Taxable distributions are not subject to the 10 percent early withdrawal penalty if the participant is 59½, dead, disabled, or taking equal periodic payments over his or her life expectancy for at least five years or until age 59½, whichever comes later, or for qualified higher education, first-time home purchase up to $10,000, and certain medical expenses.

SOURCE: USAA Investment Management Company

(Rules) of the Road to Early Retirement

▶ To retire early, your children need to become adults at the appropriate age and must learn to be financially independent. Even if you're well-off, your kids should understand the value of a dollar and should be instilled with good savings habits.

▶ Education IRAs are one investment vehicle to save for college. You might also want to consider prepaid tuition plans that are available in many states.

▶ You are permitted to put away money in an education IRA, even if you've made a full contribution to a Roth or traditional IRA.

▶ The key is not to abandon your retirement savings program to pay for college or other expenses related to children. If you can't afford to keep saving for retirement while paying for your child's expenses, you'll need to scale back your lifestyle and spend less on them.

CHAPTER 14

≈ # Déjà Vu
All Over Again

Throughout this book, suggestions have been offered on how to retire early. At the risk of oversimplification, let's summarize the advice. It's worth repeating that not every suggestion will fit with how you want to live your life. That's fine, because you don't have to follow every suggestion to retire. You can pick what works for you.

Nevertheless, certain elements of the strategy are a must. If you want to retire early or at any time in the new millennium, you must take advantage of 401(k)s and other retirement savings accounts. There are no ifs, ands, or buts about this, unless you're expecting a windfall to fund your retirement.

Put the maximum allowable amount in retirement savings plans, even if your employer doesn't match all of the contribution you make. Your employer will take out your contribution before you get your hands on it. These forced savings programs ensure that you put money away each month. Because you save automatically, no discipline or will power is necessary.

Even if you're contributing to a 401(k) or a similar retirement savings plan, don't forget about individual retirement accounts (IRAs). If your income is under the cap, you can take an immediate tax deduction for the amount contributed. If you make too much to qualify for a tax deduction, open a Roth IRA, which allows tax-free withdrawals after age 59½.

You need more than just IRAs and 401(k)s to retire early. You also need ready cash if you hope to retire before age 59½. Although there are ways to access retirement accounts before that age, those investment vehicles will normally cover the post–59½ stage of your retirement.

Unless there are survivorship issues, keep your hands off your pension, even if you can access it before age 59½. Everyone needs different types of assets to depend on. If you are scheduled to receive a fixed income for life from a defined benefit plan, even a modest one, build the rest of your investment portfolio around it. The key to reducing risk is diversification. A pension will be the conservative element of your portfolio. You can supplement it with riskier investments.

The early retirement strategy offered here does not involve tapping pensions early. Early retirement may not be everything you're expecting. There is a very real possibility that you'll want to go back to work. Because of that possibility, you shouldn't jeopardize your long-term retirement funds.

Throughout this book, the advice has been to secure the post–59½ stage of your retirement first. As a general rule, leave your retirement accounts alone until that age, even though there are ways to tap them earlier without penalty. If your retirement accounts have grown by leaps and bounds, you may be able to take substantially equal periodic withdrawals before age 59½ and still have more than enough left.

If your post–59½ needs are met, you will need cash during the transition period from your early retirement date until age 59½. Work backwards from age 59½ with the amount of cash you have on hand or expect to have in your pocket at the appropriate time. With each year's worth of savings, you can move up your early retirement date.

You have to set aside funds in bank accounts and investments that are accessible before age 59½. The most obvious answer is to increase the money you're putting away in accounts that won't penalize you for making withdrawals. With investments that aren't tax-sheltered, take advantage of the reduced capital gains rate.

Because of the Taxpayer Relief Act of 1997, the tax rate on capital gains was reduced to 20 percent for individuals and 10 percent for persons in the 15 percent tax bracket. Under the Taxpayer Relief Act of 1997, the new rate was effective for assets held at least 18 months and sold after July 28, 1997. For assets held between 12 and 18 months and sold after July 28, 1997, the 28 percent maximum rate was applicable. In 1998, Congress passed a new law that reduced the holding period to 12 months or longer. As a result, the current holding period for favorable treatment is the same as before the Taxpayer Relief Act of 1997, but the tax rate is lower.

The capital gains rate is important because some readers will need to invest aggressively if they want to retire early or have waited too long to save for retirement. You'll need lots of ready cash to bridge the gap from when the paychecks stop until you're 59½ or can start drawing a pension or receive Social Security checks. Once you're where you want to be, you're better off with a diversified portfolio, so a plunge in the market won't unretire you.

Make certain your portfolio contains a mixture of different kinds of assets. Diversify your investments among domestic stock funds that invest in large and small companies, international stock funds, and bond funds. Rebalance and make changes along the way. This is an investment strategy known as asset allocation.

More than likely, you can't avoid the stock market if you hope to retire early. Most people will need to utilize equity investments to achieve this goal. Whether it's the funds in your retirement accounts or funds you can access at any time, you need to take a certain amount of risk with your money.

As you close in on early retirement, the money you need for the first two to three years should be in conservative investments like money market funds or government bond funds. The money you won't need for five or six years should be invested more aggressively. The money from aggressive and riskier mutual funds should be gradually moved to more conservative investments. One possibility is taking the capital gains from the riskier funds and moving them to more conservative ones.

Even after you retire, a significant portion of your money needs to be in the stock market. This is especially true for early retirees who will spend decades in retirement. They can't afford to be too conservative with their investment strategy.

If you don't know how to invest, look for no-load mutual funds with low expenses. By investing the same amount at regular intervals, a strategy called dollar cost averaging, you'll minimize your risk. You'll buy more shares when prices are low and fewer shares when prices are high. Over the long haul, you'll wind up with a favorable price per share and are more likely to make a bigger profit.

You should have a long-term horizon when it comes to investing. While the value of your investments may fluctuate from day to day, you'll do well in the long run. The earlier you start, the better. By doing so, you'll take advantage of compounding. You're building from a constantly increasing principal base.

If you can't build a substantial pre–59½ account with savvy investing, there are other ways to add to your cash reserves. It might be necessary to sell that big house you own now and use the money to bridge the gap while you're waiting to access your retirement accounts. Many empty nesters are considering that possibility anyway.

Under the new tax law, a married couple of any age is permitted to take up to $500,000 of gain tax free on their primary residence. The limit for a single person is $250,000. You can take advantage of this tax break more than once, as long as you wait two years in between sales. Watch out for any state taxes that may cut into your profits.

Aside from selling your house and living on the capital gain, the new tax rules may even give you a different way to finance your early retirement. If you're a good judge of real estate and handy, you might be able to make some money. You can buy a home and fix it up. If it's been your primary dwelling for at least two years, you can take advantage of the tax break again.

There are also some great tax breaks when you rent your home. Renting your house while you're traveling or living in a vacation dwelling may more than offset your expenses. If you buy that vacation or retirement home while you're still working, the tax breaks will mean more, because your income is likely to be higher.

Part-time work may be just what the doctor ordered to keep you sharp and to keep your budget from bleeding to death. Many who hope to retire early need and want to keep making money. If you're working just for the money and aren't enjoying the work, you might as well be back at the career that made you want to retire in the first place. Early retirement is the perfect time for a transitional career that will keep you afloat until you have complete access to retirement accounts.

The best time to start planning that post-retirement career is while you're still working. Perhaps you can moonlight to explore an alternative career and boost savings. You can also start making contacts in that field or in the geographic area where you want to wind up.

A side business opens up new tax breaks. You can take advantage of the retirement plans for small business owners. Once you're retired and no longer covered by an employer's health insurance plan, you can deduct a percentage of your health insurance premiums. Until you're eligible for Medicare, you'll need a comprehensive health insurance plan that's guaranteed renewable. If you're relatively healthy, take the highest deductible you can afford to lower the cost.

As you might have feared, cutting corners is part of the quick route to retirement. The strategy involves a combination of saving more, cutting back on expenses, and living beneath your means. A key point to remember with this strategy is that you don't have to give up everything. You're just getting the best deal on those purchases you do make.

Cutting your living expenses serves a two-fold purpose. When you learn to live on less, it means you can reduce the amount you'll need per year. It also means you'll save more and will accelerate your early retirement date.

Make major purchases like a car before you retire. Although major expenditures crop up from time to time, get the ones you know about out of the way. It won't be the last car you'll purchase, hopefully, but you may be able to hold off buying another until you're able to access your retirement accounts without a penalty. If you're planning a driving vacation, it may pay to rent a car. If you're driving a considerable distance and can get unlimited mileage with the rental, the cost might be less than the depreciation on your vehicle.

Try to drive into early retirement with no debt. Clean off your credit card balances and pay your bill in full each month. Pay off your mortgage, if you can do so without wiping out the cash you need for early retirement.

At some point, you'll want to live off the earnings from your investments. If you're investing in bank certificates of deposit (CDs), they can't be tied up for years. One strategy is to ladder the maturity dates of your CDs, so they'll come due at different times when you need the money.

That's all well and good, but it puts the cart before the horse. Before you can ladder your CDs, you must purchase a good number of them. If your plan is to live off the interest and redeem them when necessary, you'll need quite a few.

You can retire early, even if you have children. But they can't be children who need your assistance forever. The earlier your children become self-reliant, the sooner you'll be able to retire. Encourage them to work part time when they're old enough. Get them started in an IRA, so they can retire early.

RETIRING SOONER, NOT LATER

More important than any strategy is having a genuine desire to retire early and be financially independent. As mentioned on too many occasions, retiring early involves delaying gratification in some facets of your life. Unless you truly want to retire early, you're likely to become sidetracked on the road to early retirement.

A Greyhound bus driver died recently in a terrible accident on the Pennsylvania Turnpike. It was his last trip before retiring after a long career with the bus company. Because it was his last trip, members of his family were aboard and also died. Around the same time, a well-known Pittsburgh attorney died in his middle sixties after a fall at the office. Closer to home for me, a 41-year-old friend died the other day from a melanoma.

The point of this book is not that you're going to die someday, so retire early. If you love your work and it gives purpose to your life, keep plugging away for as long as you can. But if there's more you want out of life than work and you're not willing to wait until the traditional age to retire, work toward the goal of retiring early instead of just going to work.

In the television series *Third Rock from the Sun,* John Lithgow's character comments, "The people on this planet trade time for money. It's almost like taking a mortgage against their life." If you're trading the precious hours of your life for money, maybe it's time to think about paying off the mortgage.

INDEX

≈